TIME WAS AWAY

Still are thy pleasant voices, thy nightingales, awake;
For Death, he taketh all away, but them he cannot take.

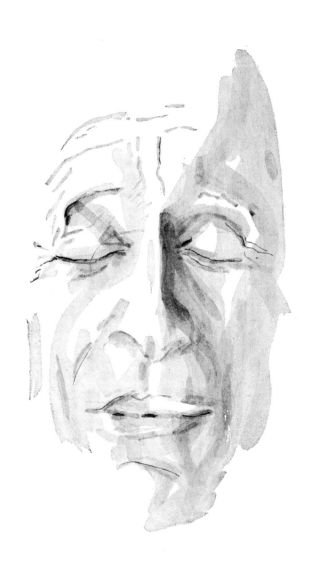

TIME WAS AWAY
The World of Louis MacNeice

edited by Terence Brown
& Alec Reid

THE DOLMEN PRESS

*Set in Times Roman type and
printed and published in the Republic of Ireland at
the Dolmen Press, North Richmond Industrial Estate,
North Richmond Street, Dublin 1*

1974

*Distributed outside Ireland, except in the U.S.A. and in Canada,
by Oxford University Press*

*General distributors in the U.S.A. and in Canada
Humanities Press Inc.,
171 First Avenue, Atlantic Highlands, N.J. 07716*

*The frontispiece is a drawing
of the poet's death mask
by his daughter
Corinna MacNeice*

ISBN 0 85105 237 1

CONTENTS

ACKNOWLEDGEMENTS

The editors wish to express their gratitude to Mrs. Hedli MacNeice for her encouragement and co-operation: to her, to Professor E. R. Dodds and to the Louis MacNeice estate; to Messrs. Faber and Faber, to Oxford University Press, New York, to Oxford University Press, London, for permission to quote from the works of Louis MacNeice. Extracts from Louis MacNeice, *The Strings are False* are used by permission of the Executors of Louis MacNeice and David Higham Associates Limited. Gratitude is also due to the late W. H. Auden, to his literary executor and to Charles Monteith Esq. for the Memorial Address. "Prologue" first appeared in *The Listener* and 'For Louis MacNeice' in *The Times Literary Supplement*.

PROLOGUE

LOUIS MacNEICE

The Romans looked the other way, the roads
Remained boreens and never ran on time;
With cattle raids and treachery, with tangled
Woods like dark intrigues, long since cut down
Only to leave intrigues, with will o' the wisps
Like un-thought-out ideals, with ragged walls
Gapped like a faulty argument, with haycocks
Sodden-grey and resigned like slaves, with cormorants
Waiting to pounce like priests, with blue hills waiting
Like women to shed their loneliness, with whins
Blazing like chronic birthdays, with explosions
Of rooks like jokes in crowded bars, with cries
Of black-faced sheep like black-faced ghosts, with tramps
Like thorn-trees walking, tattered and gnarled, with salmon
Hovering side by side, keeping position,
Headed upstream like lovers, with cairns and turf-stacks
Keeping position like hermits, with broken cliffs
Keeping position like broken heroes, with waves
Breaking upon them like time, with sunlight breaking
Sideways through the clouds like a word of God,
With grey gone amethyst, dun gone purple, green
Gone greenest yet, with rock and muck no longer
Rock and muck but light, light immanent, light transcendent,
Light that takes in all colour, then suddenly fades;
With all this flaring and fading, soaring and sinking,
Roaring and dreaming, caterwauling and song,
Day and decay, night and delight, joy and alloy,
Pros and cons, glitter and filth, this island,
Hitched to the sun that sets in the Atlantic,
Lumbers into her misty west. In vain
The Norman castle and the Tudor bribe:
The natives remained native, took their bribe
And gave their word and broke it, while the brambles

Swamped the deserted bastion. Thus today
Some country house, up to its neck in weeds,
Looks old enough to stand its ground beside
The bone-grey bog oak in the bogs. The old
Disorder keeps its pattern while the new
Order has gone stagnant, barely moving
Except for bubbles of gas or foreign insects
Skidding across the surface; in the dance-halls,
Even those in the Gaeltacht, siren voices
Ogle our mute inglorious saints and heroes
To brave the seas and join the glossy future.
Have with you to Ben Bulben! To the tourist
This land may seem a dreamland, an escape,
But to her sons and even more her daughters
A dream from which they yearn to wake; the liner
Outhoots the owls of the past. The saffron kilt
May vie with the Orange sash but the black and white
Of the press of the rest of the world scales down their feuds
To storms in a broken teacup. What is the Border
Compared with the mushroom fears of the dizzy globe
In which no borders hold? Yet at this phase
With her children either leaving and losing Ireland
Or remaining there to lose themselves, we can still
Take stock before we are silenced. What can we offer
To still make sense or leave a grateful taste?
'The Character of Ireland'? Character?
A stage convention? A historical trap?
A geographical freak? Let us dump the rubbish
Of race and talk to the point: what is a nation?
Have with you to the Post Office! Was it a nation
They gave their lives for, was it rather a gesture
That as in a poem, a play, a flourish of brushwork,
Gives meaning to an accident, in passing
Confirms what was not there? So in their passing
Did sixteen men impose upon their fellows
An unsolicited poetry? Which, needless
To say, as soon as it could relapsed to prose —
A land of priests and grocers. Here we are then,
If only for a little, asking questions
And staying, for a little, for an answer
Which well may melt in our hands. Of course there are facts,

However expurgated, inflated, doctored,
But what do they add up to? Some QED
We had not wished to demonstrate? As if
One kept the diary of a love affair
Leaving out all the part that is writ in water,
That interflow of feeling. Even so
We who were born in this land of words and water
Know that to judge a love by facts alone —
And even should the affair be ended — means
To say it never happened. Which is false.
What happened must persist. As the past persists
For all the siren voices of the liners
And, for all the standing scum in committee room and office,
Water elsewhere keeps flowing. Between the lines
Of prose we can glimpse the ripple, as through the holes
In the official mask we can catch the eye,
Clouded or clear, of one who is always one.
Facts have their place of course but should learn to keep it. The feel
Of a body is more than body. That we met
Her, not her, is a chance; that we were born
Here, not there, is a chance but a chance we took
And would not have it otherwise. The water
Flows, the words bubble, the eyes flash,
The prism retains identity, that squalor,
Those bickerings, lies, disappointments, self-deceptions.
Still dare not prove that what was love was not;
Inheritors of paradox and prism
And stigmatised to the good by the Angry Dove,
As through our soft and rain-shot air the sun
Can alchemise our granite or boulder clay,
So we, marooned between two continents
And having missed half of their revolutions
And more than half their perquisites can still,
Sophisticated primitives, aspire
In spite of all their slogans and our own
To take this accident of time and place
And somehow, even now, to make it happy.
Have with you to Maynooth or the Walls of Derry,
The Rock of Cashel or the Shannon Dam,
The vanished Claddagh or the empty Blaskets,
The Bells of Shandon, the Bog of Allen, the Boyne,

Mount Jerome or Mountjoy Prison or Croke Park,
Have with you to Lough Derg or Sandy Row,
The fuchsias of Letterfrack, the pubs of Letterkenny,
The crosses of Clonmacnois, have with you where you will
To any less heard-of places, dull grey dirty towns
Or small drab fields of ragweed, though not mentioned
In the record, even these were part of the affair
Like those off-moments when two persons feel
Their love assured because it seems so casual,
So usual, down to earth, common-or-garden,
Off-moments that are really inner moments
When they can afford to forget to say 'I love you'
And yawn and think of other things, which yet
Revolve around this absence. So the eye
Can miss the current in a stream, the ear
Ignore even a waterfall, the mind,
Intent on solid fact, forget that water,
Which early thinkers thought the source of all things,
Remains the symbol of our life; yet never,
No more than peat can turn again to forest,
No more than the die, once cast, can change its spots,
No more than a child can disavow its birthplace,
No more than one's first love can be forgotten,
If pressed, could we deny this water flows.

This poem was originally written as the prologue to a collection of essays entitled 'The Character of Ireland', edited by Louis MacNeice and W. R. Rodgers. The book was to be published by the Clarendon Press, but the editors died before the book was completed. The publishers, to whom we make acknowledgement, hope that publication may be possible at some future date.

LOUIS MAC NEICE:
A MEMORIAL ADDRESS

W. H. AUDEN

We have come together here for two purposes: to remember a person dear to us, thought of and addressed by most of us as Louis, who has just died, and to pay homage to a maker and scholar, Louis MacNeice, whose poems, translations and radio dramas many hundreds of readers who never met him admire, and many more, as yet unborn, will discover to their delight. Our mortality is seldom real to us. Even when our parents die, our primary awareness is not so much of death as of loneliness — henceforth we shall no longer be sustained by a bond which, because it was created by nature, could not be broken: from now on, our relations with others will depend, for better or worse, upon their choice and ours. But when a person of our own generation to whom we have been close, as a brother, a husband, a lover, a friend, a colleague, someone we have opened our hearts to and shared our thoughts with, someone with whom we have frequently drunk and joked together, dies suddenly, our sorrow is accompanied by terror — instead of our friend, the dead man might be you or I and, if it were so, to how many, in truth, would our absence be real? For, when death is really present to us, we cannot deceive ourselves. When a person dies, we learn the exact truth about our feelings towards him: we cannot pretend that we cared if, in fact, we were indifferent, and *vice versa*.

We all know what the word *love* ought to mean, for we all know how we should like to be loved — for ourselves as we are — but it is difficult, perhaps impossible, to love the living as we ought, because our relation to them is confused and corrupted by our own selfish envies, hopes and fears. To the degree, however, that our love for the living has been genuine, our love for the dead, in relation to whom there is no distinction between past and future, can, with God's grace, become perfect, without desire, without competition.

I should be very surprised were I to learn that Louis had any real enemies. I don't mean, of course, that he was an angelic character who never had a row with anybody or, if he did, was always entirely blameless. I mean that I do not believe there was anybody for whom to think of Louis was, automatically, to wish him ill. Not to make enemies is, in part, a matter of luck. There are people with kind and generous natures but an appearance of arrogance which arouses a hostility they do not deserve, and there are occupations, in business or politics, for example, in which a man, irrespective of his character, cannot avoid making enemies. Aside from his warm and generous nature, Louis was fortunate in that his work lay in spheres where, though meanness and ruthless ambition are, no doubt, always possible, they are not obligatory, and he was blessed with the social ability to make himself agreeable to a wide variety of human beings. I, myself, was sometimes surprised at this since I felt certain that he was, by temperament, shy and reserved, but perhaps it was this very reserve which made him such a welcome companion. He had as much respect for the solitude of others as for his own: he would never, one knew, importune intimate revelations one was unwilling to grant, nor thrust problems upon oneself.

What, then, would Louis wish for us, his friends? Firstly, surely, that, remembering him and for his sake, we should more than ever enjoy those temporal pleasures which he can no longer share with us, his pleasure in language, in country landscapes, in city streets and parks, in birds, beasts and flowers, in nice clothes, good conversation, good food, good drink, and in what he called 'the tangles'.

Secondly, that we may always find the strength to be ourselves, which, since we are not animals but human beings, means to be reborn every day. No one knew better than Louis that this is easier talked of than accomplished, that the temptations, from within and without, to surrender to what he called 'The Habits' are very strong, for the Habits promise to defend us against nightmare, the bad days when we are conscious only of failure and time frittered away, the moments in the small hours when the heart is numb with disgust at ourselves and the universe. But, if we are to be true to ourselves, we must face them, hoping that in the end we shall be able to say, as, without vanity or false modesty, Louis was able to write of himself in a recent poem:

> He was not Tom or Dick or Harry,
> Let alone God, he was merely fifty,

> No one and nowhere else, a walking
> Question but no more cheap than any
> Question or quest is cheap.
> ('The Blasphemies')

Lastly, I think he would wish that neither impatience nor despair may ever prevent us from being open at all times to those sudden visitations of joy, those moments of vision granted us by Dame Kind, or Eros, or, maybe, God Himself, moments which cannot be commanded or anticipated, but which can only be received by hearts which are open to receive them.

> The air blows in, the pigeons cross.
>   Communication! Alchemy!
> Here is profit where was loss,
>   And what was dross is golden.
> These are friends who now were foreign,
>   And gentler shines the face of doom.
> The pot of flowers inspires the window,
> The air blows in, the vistas open,
>   And a sweet smell pervades the room.
> ('The Window')

This is no occasion for a literary lecture about the poet Louis MacNeice: it is, however, fitting that I should say a few words about him as an example to other poets, present and to come. It goes without saying that every genuine poet sees life from a unique perspective and that what we find in his poems we can find no-where else. This uniqueness is a must, but we also hope, though we have no right to demand it, that each new poem he writes shall not only delight but also surprise, so that, if it were unsigned, we might not immediately recognise its author. If the adjective 'minor' has any real meaning when applied to a poet, is it not that, in his work, this element of surprise, of development over the years, is lacking? His poems may be very beautiful and original but, comparing one with another, it is hard to guess, on the evidence of the poems themselves, which was written first. Louis MacNeice was clearly a poet who shared Cesare Pavese's belief that 'the only joy in life is to begin', that, from the poet's point of view, the excitement of tackling a problem, whether of technique or subject matter, which one has never attempted before, is even more important than the result. I am confident that posterity will sustain my conviction that his

later poems show an advance upon his earlier, are more certain
in their craftsmanship, brilliant though that always was, and more
moving; but, even if I thought otherwise, I should still admire him
for risking failure rather than being content to repeat himself
successfully.

In this age, to die at fifty-five is, statistically speaking, to die
early, but worse things can befall a poet than an early death. At
least, Louis MacNeice was spared that experience which some
poets have had to endure, and for many years: the experience of
being condemned to go on living with the knowledge that the Muse
has abandoned them. Not only was his Muse faithful to him till
the end, but she had increased her favours, and we can truthfully
say of him what, in an elegy, he wrote of a friend:

> . . . the fact remains
> (Which I, for all your doubts can have no doubt of)
> That your whole life till then showed an endeavour
> Towards a discovery. . . .
>
> ('The Casualty')

Every poet knows that, when he looks back over what he has
written, the poems it is a torment and a shame to recall are not
those which, for one reason or another, were failures — no poet
who writes much can hope to escape writing some poems which are
bad or, at least, boring — but those which he knows to be clever
forgeries, expressing feelings or attitudes which were not really his,
but which vanity, a wish to please an audience, or the wrong kind
of conscience deluded him into fancying were genuine. Of these he
is, very rightly, ashamed, because he cannot say 'I should have
written it differently' or 'It was the best I could do at the time':
he can only say 'I ought never to have written it, and I needn't
have.'

Of all the poets of his generation and mine, I would say without
hesitation that Louis MacNeice had the least cause for self-
reproach, and his example denies to the rest of us the excuse that,
in the historical circumstances under which we grew up, the temptations to fake feelings were unusually strong, true though this may
be: Louis MacNeice's work is a proof that they could be resisted.

No poet can know for whom he is writing and, of those persons
whose verdict would mean most to him, the majority are dead.
While he was alive, I cared a great deal what Louis MacNeice
thought of what I wrote: now it will be impossible for me to write

anything without feeling that he is looking over my shoulder, and without invoking his protection against those demons of *bêtise* and falsehood which are always lying in wait for an unguarded moment to ensnare one in some new folly.

Anyone who has moved in literary circles knows how vain so many writers are, how envious and malicious about each other, and that these defects are not confined to those who have failed to receive critical or popular acclaim, in whom they are understandable. One can, unfortunately, encounter writers who are deservedly famous, yet cannot say a good word for a colleague or bear to hear him praised in their presence. How many, too, when a colleague publishes a poor work, rejoice in his discomfiture. In this kind of vanity and envy, Louis MacNeice was totally lacking. I don't mean that he was uncritical — his standards were very high — but he judged others by the same standards as he judged himself, he always hoped that others would write something he could admire, and he was delighted when they did.

Of persons in many walks of life, to say of them that they exhibited the bourgeois virtues of financial probity and social responsibility would seem impertinent, something to be taken for granted; but, in the case of a poet, I believe it is not. Since no poet, simply by practising the vocation to which he believes he has been called, can earn his daily bread, he is more tempted than the majority of men to fancy that the world owes him a living. He may succumb to this completely and become a sponger who relies on others to support him, or he may partially succumb, that is to say, while taking a job to earn a living, refuse to be conscientious about what he is paid to do. As all who were colleagues of Louis MacNeice, whether as fellow teachers or as fellow workers at the B.B.C., will testify, he gave of his best to whatever task he was given, whether he enjoyed it or, as must sometimes have happened, he found it a dreary chore. When it can be said of a poet that, without in any way sacrificing his artistic integrity to Mammon, he sponged on no one, he cheated no one, he provided for his family, and he paid his bills, these facts, I consider, deserve to be recorded.

Some poets have consciously written their own epitaphs. Louis MacNeice did not, but these lines, surely, might well be written on his tomb:

> Live men and dead
> Being each unique
> (Their pain and glory),

> Yet some will have left
> By force or freak
> To us the bereft
> Some richer story;
> Their say being said,
> They still can speak
> Words more unique,
> More live, less dead.
>
> ('Visitations')

Or, as descriptive both of Louis our friend and Louis MacNeice the maker, these:

> The man with the shy smile has left behind
> Something that was intact.
>
> ('The Suicide')

TREES WERE GREEN

ELIZABETH NICHOLSON

On the last Christmas Eve of his life, my brother Louis said to me: 'You and I, Elizabeth, remember so much about our childhoods, yet we seem to remember such different things.' We agreed that this was so, in that while (as he said himself) 'not forgetting the moments of glory', Louis's memories were much more predominantly sombre. He would, I think, if questioned have said that his early childhood was unhappy. Coming from the same household, mine though containing its sorrows was basically happy.

This difference in outlook stemmed partly from the fact that the first ten years of my life were irradiated by the warmth and love and vitality of my mother. When she began to be ill Louis was only five and his memories of her before that time were fragmentary and shadowy, at least so he said.

> In my childhood trees were green
> And there was plenty to be seen.
> ('Autobiography')

Although I remember Louis from the day he was born, he first comes into memory as a child old enough to be a play-companion at about the time in early 1911 that the family moved into the Rectory which was situated just outside the little town that Carrickfergus then was. We had always before lived in streets. Now suddenly we were in another world with a lawn to play on, trees to climb, and a garden which seemed to be full of apple-blossom. And I have never forgotten the thrill of surprise on the first morning when I woke up to the dawn chorus. At this time I was eight and Louis three-and-a-half. Our mongol brother, Willie, came in between us but was not really a companion as he had not yet learnt to talk.

My mother was very pleased by this move. All her instincts were of the country and she began at once enlarging the henyard, planting rose trees, acquiring cats and dogs and hens and so on.

[11]

Both Louis and I took interest in these activities and Louis in particular spent much time with his mother. I went out to day-school, and Willie lived largely in the nursery, but our mother kept Louis with her in the kitchen and used to take him with her when she went shopping or visiting in the parish. Miss MacCready (Miss Craig of *The Strings are False*) came soon after our move but was not nearly so important in our lives at this time as she was after-wards to become.

My mother had a talent for producing a placid, orderly kind of household and we soon became settled into a quiet rhythm which was very satisfying, I think, to both Louis and myself. Although we lived only just outside Carrickfergus, the environment was a rural one. The North Road on which the Rectory stood climbed steadily upwards into a country of low hills and small farms. Our milkman's cows passed twice daily, journeying between their grazing fields and the byre behind his house in the town. We were always interested to see them file in through his front door. And on market days a slow procession of the orange carts mentioned in 'Valediction' would pass our gate. The fields around were not then built up and were full of corncrakes, and the days seemed filled with country activities — setting hens in the lamp pantry in spring, haymaking on a small scale in summer, and in autumn the apples to pick, after which we used to 'spread the shining crop on the spare room floor' (*The Dark Tower*). The house ticked with the seasons, and we kept up all the traditional ceremonies. We picked mayflowers on May Eve, we rolled eggs in the fields on Easter Monday, my mother taught us all the Hallowe'en games and provided the right foods, and both father and mother felt Christmas so deeply in a religious sense that Christmas Day really was a day of joy and friendliness when no one would ever have thought of quarrelling or even speaking sharply. Louis never lost this reverence for Christmas and to the end of his life he tried year after year to recreate the spirit of those early Rectory Christmases, often, I am afraid, sad because he never quite could.

So long as she remained well, our mother had a great capacity for the enjoyment of life which, I think, she handed on to Louis. She was always thinking of enchanting things to do with us, and she entered at once and entirely into all our joys and sorrows. I remember, too, how her feet never failed to tap to a dance tune, and she persuaded my father to let me go to dancing classes (a fact which I remembered later with bitterness when my very kind but

Puritan stepmother forbade all dancing more or less as a work of the devil).

My father made the walls resound,
He wore his collar the wrong way round.

We saw a good deal less of our father because he was so much taken up with his work, but so long as our mother was there, I don't think that either of us was afraid of him. He could not enter into a child's mind as our mother did, but she somehow formed a channel of communication between him and ourselves and there had not grown up as yet the awe with which we later came to regard him.

Later on, after my mother's death, both Louis and I became afraid of arousing his disapproval. We never doubted his deep affection for us and we knew that he was always concerned for our welfare, but he could somehow appear awe-inspiring and at times stern when he may not even have realised that he was producing this effect. What seemed to us anger was often, I think, only impatient annoyance at childish tiresomeness. He was not at ease with children and he was inclined to expect from us a degree of responsibility which we were not yet mature enough to give. He seemed to us to walk in a remote and different world and his rare incursions into ours were unpredictable: for example, he would suddenly express annoyance at some activity which had been going on openly and unchecked for some time past and which he had probably only just noticed. I am certain that he felt just as unhappy and guilty about this breakdown of communications as we did.

However, in 1911 our mother was still there and we were happy and at ease with both parents. In fact, in that first year at the Rectory 'the trees were green' and if I had to find an epigram to sum it up in my memory, I think it would be 'Hadn't we the gaiety.' It was early in 1912 that the dark shadows began, at first gradually, to invade all our lives.

My mother wore a yellow dress;
Gently, gently, gentleness.

Even in these early sunlit days there was a kind of tension in the household which, I think, arose in part from the fact that neither our mother nor Louis nor I myself felt that we belonged properly to the Ulster community in which we were living. Our parents had both been born and spent their childhoods in Connemara. Our father had chosen to work in the North and although he always remained a Western Irishman, he grew to love the Northern people whom he served in spite of the fact that his political opinions differed widely from theirs. Our mother was thirty-five when she married and came to the North, and her first home there was in Ballymacarett in East Belfast where she must have come straight up against the more dour and bigoted inhabitants of that city. Had she lived there longer than she did, she would probably (as happened in Carrickfergus) have recognised the generosity of nature which the dourness so often masks. However, accustomed only to the gentler speech and ways of Dublin and Connemara, she developed a frank dislike of the North of Ireland which she retained for the rest of her life. After they first went to Carrickfergus in 1908, my parents experienced a good deal of hostility for about a year, not for personal reasons, but because the parishioners had wished the existing curate to be appointed as Rector. But by the time of the move to the Rectory, all this was past and both parents had become loved and valued by nearly everybody. Our mother in her turn began to understand the people better and she made good friends, but by and large, she still disliked the Ulster atmosphere. My father occasionally told us stories of Connemara, but my mother spoke of it so constantly and with such love and such longing that I think it was she who really made it come alive for Louis and myself. It became for us both a 'many-coloured land', a kind of lost Atlantis where we thought that by rights we should be living, and it came to be a point of honour that we did not belong to the North of Ireland. We were in our minds a West of Ireland family exiled from our homeland.

Our mother was undoubtedly largely responsible for this conflict of identities. She tried hard (though unsuccessfully) to prevent us from acquiring the Ulster accent and dialect which we heard all around us. Incidentally, both she and my father were in different ways purists about language. This may in part have helped to produce the ease of expression and facility for juggling with words which Louis later possessed to such a marked degree. My father had a scholar's interest in words, their derivation and so on, and he was very particular about choosing them accurately to convey meaning. My mother took emotional likes and dislikes to the sound of words and would not allow us to use those which she disliked. It is perhaps worth noting that our father was able at a moment's notice to produce quite respectable doggerel verse on any given subject, and would occasionally carry on a rhyming correspondence with various friends.

The second year at the Rectory, 1912, opened well. It was in that spring that one day we were taken for a walk up the hill to a point where we could catch

> . . . one shining glimpse
> Of a boat so big it was named Titanic
> ('Death of an Old Lady')

as she passed down the lough on her trial trip.

In June my mother took all three children for a holiday to Portstewart. She had already begun from time to time to have attacks of physical illness which confined her to bed, and in hindsight, I think that the beginning of her mental disturbance was perhaps already there. She was not so cheerful as usual and almost every day she took us to some rocks. We played about while she would sit for hours as if fascinated, watching the endless surge and crash of the Atlantic rollers.

It was in September of this year that our father made history by being one of the few Protestants in the North of Ireland who refused to sign the Ulster Covenant for reasons of conscience. The Carrickfergus Orangemen asked for a service in the parish church before going up to Belfast to sign the covenant, some of them in blood. My father provided the service and preached a brave sermon in which he said that each man must follow his own conscience but that for himself he could not pledge unconditional obedience to any measures which the leaders might call for. And he spoke out as always against the use of violence. As Mr. Tommy Robinson, the butcher, said on leaving the church: 'That was a grand sermon the Rector gave us. But he spoilt it all at the end by telling us he wasn't going to sign the covenant.'

And yet, however much they deprecated his views, my father never lost the affection of his parishioners, an affection which only deepened with the years. Louis was just five at this time; there was so much talk in the house about Carson and the covenant that he must have heard it though he never in later years seemed to have memory of doing so. Of course, he heard the history of it later on.

It is perhaps of topical interest to note here that when Lord Carson died, my father wrote me a letter in which after paying tribute to various points which he could esteem in Carson's character, he went on to say: 'But he will be remembered as the man who broke the unity of Ireland.'

> When I was five the black dreams came;
> Nothing after was quite the same.

Around Christmas, my mother was ill in bed but recovered and seemed much as usual. One morning in February she went up to Belfast for the day. When she left the house, she was herself, our everyday, comforting mother. She came back that evening in tears and although it was to be another six months before we finally lost her physical presence in the house, nothing after that day 'was quite the same'. She had visited a gynaecologist who had told her that she must have an almost immediate hysterectomy, and this news seemed to trigger off the agitated depression from which she never again really emerged.

I know from hearing my mother talk with her friends that she quite mistakenly believed that Louis's difficult birth had in some way caused the uterine fibroid from which she suffered. It is probable that Louis also heard this talk and from passages in his poetry and remarks made in later life, I believe that he had an irrational idea, perhaps only partly conscious, that his birth had caused his mother's later illness and death.

In March, my mother went off to Belfast and had her entirely successful operation. We were taken to see her in the nursing-home and told that she was getting better and would soon be back. She came back but she was still in depression. She was at home all that summer and seemed to be nearly always sad and crying. A nurse came to stay in the house and nearly every afternoon a hired phaeton used to come to take my mother for drives. She and the nurse would sit on the main seat and one child was always taken to sit on the little seat facing them. I don't know what Louis felt on these drives. I enjoyed them, but at the same time the scenery became intermingled with my mother's sorrow. We used often to pass within sight of a little house far in the distance in the hills; I thought that it was like a face and the windows were eyes full of tears and it always looked like this to me in later life.

My mother had been trained as a schoolmistress by the Society for Irish Church Missions. Her temperament was the reverse of

Calvinistic but her early education was probably much influenced by Calvinist ideas. As so many depressed people do, she developed ideas of having committed unforgivable sins and was inclined to talk even to the children about Death and Judgement, Hell and Heaven and kindred subjects. I certainly heard this talk, and I think that Louis must have done so also. We were both constantly with her. My father, who hated hell-fire religion, tried to comfort and reason with his wife, but it is after all impossible to reason with the disturbed mind.

Finally, in August 1913, it was decided that my mother should go to a nursing-home kept by a friend in Dublin. What was to be her last day at home came round. We were playing in the garden that morning and Louis and I, for some reason, wanted to fix a stick and some rope together in some especial way. We could not do it and appealed to my mother. Still practical and good with her hands, she was doing what we had asked her when Miss MacCready (who latterly had come to speak to our mother as if to a child) came out and said quite sharply to her: 'What are you doing there?' 'I don't know,' replied Mother, 'the children asked me to', and she went into the house to get ready to leave. She gave last injunctions to Miss MacCready and Annie. Our unpractical father was not to be asked questions about our clothes or food or health, for he would not know the answers; they were to use their own good judgment and were always to give us plenty of milk. Then some friends who owned one of the still fairly rare motor-cars of the neighbourhood arrived to drive my father and mother to the Dublin train. All three of us stood at the gate and waved our mother away, and we never saw her again.

Come back early or never come.

At first, we took it for granted that our mother would return. Louis's sixth birthday was very soon after she left and she sent him presents, and for some time she used to write me sad little letters to which I replied with messages from my brothers. Then her letters stopped and I was told that I must stop writing too until she was better. As corroborated by someone who used to visit it at that time, the Rectory became very sad. We saw less and less of my father, and when we did see him he seemed withdrawn into a sad silence. At this time he wrote to a friend: 'When I see the children playing and laughing, I know that I should rejoice, and I do too but sometimes their laughter almost shocks me.' No one talked much about our mother but for a long time I myself, and I think also Louis, were always expecting her return. I still went out and about to tea-parties and so on, but Louis became much more shut-in than before in the nursery with Miss MacCready and Willie.

Miss MacCready was as thorough a Northerner as our mother was a Southerner, and I think if we had been Ulster children by blood as well as by birth there would have been a greater degree of understanding between her and ourselves. As it was, we were bewildered and chilled by her at times almost savage humour, and took remarks seriously which were not really meant unkindly. By ordinary English standards, Miss MacCready's character would be incomprehensible, but she was not at all atypical of many people in the North of Ireland then and now. She exhibited all the outward dourness and what the late Dr. Ian Suttie has called the 'taboo on tenderness' which characterise so many of the people of the province. She tried to bring us up as she had been brought up herself and would slap us and box our ears much as a cat will cuff her kittens. At the same time, had real physical danger which she could understand menaced us, I have no doubt whatever that she would have protected us if need be with her life. Louis once in my presence having recounted some particularly hair-raising anecdote about her to a suitably wide-eyed and horrified English friend ended up by saying, 'And yet, you know, she was a good person.' And our dear Annie, writing to me about her not so very long ago, said, 'She was awful good to yous children.'

Of course, even at this time it was not all gloom. Miss MacCready fairly often took us down to the sea where she was surprisingly good-tempered and tolerant in allowing us to bathe and paddle and play much as we liked. As soon as he could write at all, at about the age of seven, Louis found, I think, considerable release in writing his first poems. And at about the same age he learned to read and we had plenty of books — we had fairy stories and so on of our own, and we were allowed quite considerable latitude in reading the books belonging to our father. And we both found a great deal of solace in playing the game of Mac Miss.

This game was very important to us both. I know that in *The Strings are False* Louis uses the spelling MacMisque and has also altered the name of his *alter ego* from Keddy to Teddy Bock. But reminiscing together in later life, we always spoke these names as I have written them, and I think that Louis must have made the alterations deliberately to mask the obvious parallelism with our own names.

I think I may have begun the game by inventing the Great Queen (or Mrs.) Mac Miss, but Louis's imagination soon took over and a whole host of invisible people came to live in the trees and bushes and sheds. They rarely came into the house. We spent hours conversing with them and even asked their advice though I cannot now remember by what means the oracle replied. Curiously, we did not keep this game particularly secret and even spoke of these personages publicly by name. I possess a volume of Hans Andersen's fairy tales (stories which Louis read and re-read) given by an adult friend and inscribed on the fly-leaf: 'To Freddy from Keddy Bock.' Incidentally, Louis was always called Freddy from his first name until he chose to change to his second when he was in his last year at Marlborough. He was christened Frederick Louis, Frederick after his father and Louis after his godfather, Mr. Louis Plunkett.

> The chilly sun
> Saw me walk away alone.

Our mother died in Dublin of tuberculosis in December, 1914, but the house continued to be her house and its ways on the whole her ways until 1917 when my father remarried and both Louis and I went to school in England. No children could have had a kinder or more generous stepmother, and Louis in particular became very fond of her. But although we both regarded her with affection, we had few interests in common with her. She had had a very strict Evangelical upbringing, far more restricted, I think, than that of either our father or mother, and she introduced a Puritan spirit into the house. She and my father often approved or disapproved of different things, but where taboos were concerned each loyally backed up the other and this led to restrictions which my father alone would not have imposed.

After Louis and I went to school in 1917 our paths increasingly diverged. We each formed new friends and interests, and the difference in age became more divisive than it had been earlier. I went to school a term before Louis. It was during the First War and for some time before I went we had played at constructing a military camp modelled on the one which we could see across the road from our house. I came back from school a bossy little girl, very pleased with myself and my new experiences and feeling very grown-up. Louis and I sat in a tree and he then asked me to come and see the improvements in the camp. To my everlasting remorse I replied, 'I don't think I want to play at the camp any more.' Louis burst into tears exactly as he had done some years earlier when Miss MacCready threw his diary, his first literary creation, into the nursery fire. I realised too late how Louis, left companionless at home, had planned the improvements to please and surprise me. I did revert to the childish game and we both played at it happily for some time later. But the wounding words had been spoken and could never be recalled.

It was during his last year at Marlborough that I think Louis began to feel really isolated from his family. No one of us really shared his intellectual and aesthetic interests or could meet him on his own ground. My father, devoted to Tennyson and Browning, could not at this time understand what Louis was trying to say in his poetry, though he came to appreciate it better later on.

Louis increasingly walked away alone, but he continued always to correspond with and to visit his family quite often. And to the very end of his life, in spite of all the tensions and ambivalence, he looked back on the pre-1917 days in Carrickfergus Rectory with a nostalgic affection which he himself expressed in one of his very last broadcasts, 'Memories of Childhood'.

MACNEICE: FATHER AND SON

TERENCE BROWN

Pride in your history is pride
In living what your fathers died,
Is pride in taking your own pulse
And counting in you someone else.

('Suite for Recorders')

In 1932 John Frederick MacNeice published a short pamphlet of sermons in Dublin, the city where he had been a university student. In this he stated:

I call Ireland our beloved country. No man is to be more pitied than the man who has no country, or the man who is not sure what his country is.

In January 1934 his son Louis MacNeice, who at twenty-six years of age was making a literary reputation in England, wrote a long poem 'Valediction' in which he took his leave of Ireland:

I will exorcise my blood
And not to have my baby-clothes my shroud
I will acquire an attitude not yours
And become as one of your holiday visitors,
And however often I may come
Farewell, my country, and in perpetuum.

The two quotations suggest the gulf that had developed between father and son and between their separate worlds.

The poet's father, John Frederick MacNeice, was a remarkable man. His stature in the Ireland of his day was considerable and his memory is still alive in the Ulster whose problems today are so similar to those with which he wrestled through most of his life. He had been born of humble parents in the West of Ireland. His father had worked as a schoolteacher on the isle of Omey, and had

[21]

been associated with an extremely zealous missionary society, the Society for Irish Church Missions. This organization was evangelical in its outlook, fundamentalist theologically and Unionist in its politics. John Frederick MacNeice attended Trinity College, Dublin, where he graduated in 1895 with high academic honours. His churchmanship differed greatly from his father's as his politics must also have done, for he became known as a clergyman with definite liberal views and as a Home Ruler in politics.

He was appointed rector of Carrickfergus parish church in 1909 when Louis was not yet two years old. It was to be a turbulent and difficult period in his life for in the space of a few years the family, already burdened by the birth of a mongoloid child, was to lose its mother, and to find itself in the midst of political developments in Ulster and in Ireland that threatened widespread civil war and national disaster.

When John MacNeice was appointed rector the first tremors of the Home Rule crisis were already being felt. Legend has it that when he officiated at morning prayer on the first Sunday of his incumbency as rector in Carrickfergus the men in his congregation remained standing with their hats on their heads in protest at his appointment instead of a local contender for the post. Be that as it may, it would have been difficult enough for a Church of Ireland clergyman from the South to have made himself completely acceptable in a town like Carrickfergus, without the developments of 1912 and 1913. John Frederick MacNeice has left a record of the occurrences in these momentous years when the Ulster Volunteers were established to oppose Home Rule by force of arms. He is writing of 1913, as the crisis deepened. It was the year in which his first wife died:

> The situation became more serious every month. In Ulster it was indeed a wonderful time. Every county had its organisation: every town and district had its corps. The young manhood of Ulster enlisted and went into training. Men of all ranks and occupations met together in the evenings for drill. There resulted a great comradeship. Barriers of class were broken down or forgotten. Protestant Ulster became a fellowship. On Saturdays there were marches, manoeuvres, competitions. . . . On Sundays colours were dedicated, and drum-head services were held when ministers of religion, of high rank in their commissions, gave their blessing.

John MacNeice, however, convinced of the justice and good sense of the Home Rule policy, had refused to sign the Ulster Covenant, and had preached a brave sermon advising restraint, unhappily meeting with little response and support from his parishioners and fellow-townspeople. Louis MacNeice recreates this period in *Autumn Journal* as one of communal hysteria:

> And I remember, when I was little, the fear
>   Bandied among the servants
> That Casement would land at the pier
>   With a sword and a horde of rebels;
> And how we used to expect, at a later date,
>   When the wind blew from the west, the noise of shooting
> Starting in the evening at eight
>   In Belfast in the York Street district;
> And the voodoo of the Orange bands
>   Drawing an iron net through darkest Ulster. . . .

The Volunteers were of course to fight not in Ulster but in France and John MacNeice records in one of his books that 133 men from the town never returned to the Ireland that began her own bitterly fought battles in the 'twenties. At this time too he was in the vanguard of those counselling moderation and tolerance — he wrote to the papers, preached against violence and sought always to prevent the adoption of irreconcilable positions.

A measure of stability restored to Ireland, two new states founded, John MacNeice settled into his career in the Church of Ireland. He became an Archdeacon and then Bishop of Cashel, finally acceding to the episcopacy of Down, Connor and Dromore. His occupancy of these posts was accompanied by no diminution of his intellectual energies, nor of his public zeal. His published sermons and papers are quite remarkable for the frank independence of mind that they express. His opinions were his own, and were often unfashionably forthright. He was a staunch supporter of the secular as opposed to the religious control of Irish education, arguing,

> Have we so little faith in the Christian religion as to think . . .
> that respect for the Christian religion will disappear if clergy-
> men cease to be school managers.

In 1929 he published a study of the ecumenical movement in South India and made a plea for the development of inter-church relations in Ireland, wishing to break the sectarian moulds of Irish life. In the 1930's he preached many sermons analysing political and social trends in the international community, pointing out to his Northern Irish listeners (no doubt many of them unable to lift their eyes from the quarrels of the Belfast streets):

> No European nation is now an independent economic unit. We are all in the same bundle of life. . . . Troubles in India mean distress in Lancashire, and distress in Lancashire creates problems that cannot be solved in an isolated way. Labour conditions in Japan help to determine the standard of life for the Belfast artisans.

He preached staunchly in support of the League of Nations, denouncing the human waste of war, but was not, even early in the 'thirties unaware of the threat which both Hitler and Stalin posed to European society:

> Thirteen years after the Armistice there are in one of the foremost countries of the world millions of unemployed. In the existing conditions there is the possibility of the downfall of Western civilization.

It was not only the son who felt

> We shall go down like palaeolithic man
> Before some new Ice Age or Genghiz Khan,
> ('An Eclogue for Christmas')

and that what must remain is

> Hatred of hatred, assertion of human values
> Which is now your only duty.
> ('Eclogue from Iceland')

John Frederick MacNeice also urged social justice for the working classes in his sermons assuming that 'the poor, the workers, the men who toil with their hands must be regarded as entitled to a fuller life than they have known hitherto' and denouncing with real moral passion the fact that

> our looms are idle, our workshops are empty, our unemployed millions aimlessly walk the streets, while there is a great multitude never accurately numbered, of broken men — the blinded, the maimed, the paralysed. . . .

As a response to the conditions of the working classes he preached in favour of workers' representation on Boards of Directors. Behind these pronouncements, throughout, was John MacNeice's Christian faith. He was first and foremost a churchman, believing that the church could have a significant rôle in world and in local politics. His vision was of the City of God, and from this flowed the analyses which make his writings remarkable documents of their time. For few other Church of Ireland clergymen in the first decades of the century had anything like John Frederick MacNeice's breadth of mind and elasticity of outlook. He had immense pride in the Church of Ireland, believing it to be the authentic church in Ireland with the apostolic succession from St. Patrick, and delighted to state

> No authority outside the shores of Ireland is recognised by her. She is in Ireland, she is of Ireland, she is for Ireland. Free from all State and political entanglements she can . . . give her best to Ireland.

Such was the poet's father, a man of courage, patriotism, commitment and faith. He was also, although a staunch puritan (teetotalism reigned in his rectory and palace), a man of general culture and no little historical knowledge. His sermons frequently dealt in Irish history, while his monograph *Carrickfergus and Its Contacts* draws on historical and literary sources, quoting the Irish poet Samuel Ferguson, the translator Standish O'Grady, as well as citing historical studies. John Hilton, the poet's friend, has left a brief pen-portrait of the churchman:

> His stalwart frame bore a massive head with the long upper lip of the archetypal Irishman and a strong development of muscles beside the mouth. . . .

The father's world, however, was not one within which the son felt he could develop personally and imaginatively. Louis MacNeice broke with his family when he was a young man, rejecting over a period of time both his father's religion and his country, choosing to live and work in England, and to maintain a position of tense scepticism about the Christian faith throughout his life. Yet over and over again in his writings Louis MacNeice turns to the figure of his father, exploring his relationship with him, defining and re-defining his memories of him and their significance for his present experience.

In his twenties Louis MacNeice was much irritated by his father and his father's world. A wider, more stimulating *milieu* had opened up to him at Marlborough and Oxford, a *milieu* more likely to suit his developing taste for elegance, style, dash and wit, than the austere world of moral concern which the rectory in Carrickfergus represented for him. In his autobiographical fragment, *The Strings Are False*, which MacNeice wrote in 1940 (and suppressed, prob-ably for fear of the hurt it might do his father and stepmother) he describes a holiday trip he took with his father to Norway and the fjords. He had returned from Oxford and Mariette (the Jewish girl he was to marry) to the Carrickfergus rectory:

> Going home that summer I found it duller than usual. Mariette might measure her life by dance-cards, keeping them in a lavendered box tied with ribbon at the bottom of a drawer, but was it any better to measure by Collects for the Day? I was detailed to accompany my father on a pleasure trip up the coast of Norway; a huge boat packed with middle-aged Americans and with English spinsters who were blowing their savings. I talked to hardly anyone on board, read John Stuart Mill's *Logic* and medieval Latin poetry. When everyone was in bed I would stand on the upper deck under the midnight sun and recite one of these poems, the "Nun's Lament". It seemed to me very appropriate.

One doubts if it would have seemed so to John Frederick MacNeice. A poem written in 1928 expressed MacNeice's irritation with the dull family life he felt he must reject. Its tone is cynical, tired. 'Happy Families' opens

> The room is all a stupid quietness,
> Cajoled only by the fire's caress;
> We loll severally about and sit
> Severally and do our business severally. . . .

The poem indicts a reunited family for its complacent respectability:

No one deserted, no one was a loafer,
Nobody disgraced us, luckily for us
No one put his foot in it or missed the bus . . .

and ends with a petulant cock of the snook:

But that's not all there is to it.

MacNeice did not return again in poetry to his immediate family background until September 1940, though poems such as 'Belfast' (1931), 'Carrickfergus' (1937), and Section XVI of *Autumn Journal* explore his roots in Ulster, while his translation of the *Agamemnon*, published in 1936, was dedicated to his father. In September 1940, however, he wrote the delicately haunting lyric 'Autobiography'. Perhaps he was working on *The Strings are False* when he produced this poem, for it contains some of the same terror of his father and his father's religion that the fragment records. Nightmares, like some of the terrible dreams that MacNeice describes in the prose work, are suggested throughout the poem (as they were in the earlier 'Intimations of Mortality').

'The Kingdom', written in 1943, introduces a new note of affection and respect. Written to celebrate individuals whom MacNeice admires, 'The Kingdom' posits an invisible underground of the truly elect who

have eyes
And can see each other's goodness, do not need salvation
By whip, brochure, sterilisation or drugs,
Being incurably human. . . .

MacNeice includes his father in their ranks in a passage of moving reconsideration set at the funeral service (John Frederick MacNeice died in 1942):

All is well with
One who believed and practised and whose life
Presumed the Resurrection. What that means
He may have felt he knew; this much is certain —

The meaning filled his actions, made him courteous
And lyrical and strong and kind and truthful,
A generous puritan.

The 1940s were a difficult time for MacNeice. He had left behind
his 'twenties when his brilliant reputation had been established. The
Depression of the 'thirties, the war, and particularly the blitz on
London had sharpened his awareness of the need for his poetry to
move on from its surfaces of bright particulars, its

Flowers in the sun beside the jewelled water.
('Mayfly')

Those, in his youth, had seemed enough to live by. The endless
flux of phenomena had satisfied his urge towards meaning. It had
been enough to live where

. . . the street fountain blown across the square
Rainbow-trellises the air and sunlight blazons
The red butcher's and scrolls of fish on marble slabs,
Whistled bars of music crossing silver sprays
And horns of cars, touché, touché, rapiers' retort, a moving
cage,
A turning page of shine and sound, the day's maze.
('Morning Sun')

As he grew older, however, the need to make some more complete
statement began to concern him. He now realized that

Because the velvet image
Because the lilting measure,
No more convey my meaning
I am compelled to use
Such words as disabuse
My mind of casual pleasure
And turn it towards a centre.
(Introductory poem 'To Hedli')

He had sensed duties and responsibilities as Britain faced up to the
prospect of a protracted war with Fascist Germany and he had left
the safety of the United States where he might have remained as a

university teacher, to return to a London suffering the blitz (although he stoutly defended his friend W. H. Auden's decision to remain in America). England and the metropolis had allowed him the freedom to explore his own sensibility, to discover and celebrate the rich diversity of experience without the necessity to judge and prepare always intruding, as it did in his father's world. The opening stanzas of 'Woods' (1946) acknowledge this, comparing England with the Ireland his father knew:

> My father who found the English landscape tame
> Had hardly in his life walked in a wood,
> Too old when first he met one; Malory's knights,
> Keats's nymphs or the Midsummer Night's Dream
> Could never arras the room, where he spelled out True and
>   Good
> With their interleaving of half-truths and not-quites.
>
> While for me from the age of ten the socketed wooden gate
> Into a Dorset planting, into a dark
> But gentle ambush, was an alluring eye;
> Within was a kingdom free from time and sky. . . .

But the poem concludes by admitting

> Yet in using the word tame my father was maybe right,
> These woods are not the Forest . . .

and with images of an English domesticity and rationality which knows nothing of the 'wilds of Mayo' and 'the Neolithic night', nothing of his father's perhaps more fundamental world except in 'inconsequent wild roses' which bloom in the midst of

> An ordered open air long ruled by dyke and fence,
> With geese whose form and gait proclaim their consequence,
> Pargetted outposts, windows browed with thatch. . . .

That there were sustaining values in his father's world was admitted as the poet concurrently sought to purge his poetry of its surface glitter and 'turn it towards a centre' that might comprehend and contain both the style and fragile elegance of the Midsummer Night's Dream and the dark energies of the 'Neolithic night' of Co. Mayo.

MacNeice wrote two other poems about his father, both of which further explore the respect he increasingly felt for him. 'The Strand' (1945) has the poet on a West of Ireland strand remembering walking there with his father. He places his father's figure firmly in the landscape suggesting a man who belonged, and knew it, even in the midst of the flux which his son had celebrated and begun to fear:

> my steps repeat

> Someone's who now has left such strands for good
> Carrying his boots and paddling like a child,
> A square black figure whom the horizon understood —

> My father.

The poem is powerfully suggestive of the impermanence of life, the endless mysteriousness of change; the mood is austerely poignant (the complicated *terza rima* rhyme scheme saves it from any sentimentality):

> It was sixteen years ago he walked this shore

> And the mirror caught his shape which catches mine
> But then as now the floor-mop of the foam
> Blotted the bright reflections — and no sign

> Remains of face or feet when visitors have gone home.

Yet the image of a man rooted in time and place remains with a poet who increasingly, as his life progressed, felt himself truly at home nowhere. There is a note of admiration and personal pain in the line

> A square black figure whom the horizon understood.

'The Truisms' is a short trenchant poem in which MacNeice, late in his life, explored for the last time in poetry the significance and the meaning that his father's world held for him. In this poem he perhaps achieves the greatest clarity and degree of resolution that he could manage on a subject that was a difficult one for him. One critic, D. B. Moore, in his book *The Poetry of Louis MacNeice*, has suggested that this poem is satiric in intent. I think this is both to misread this poem and to neglect the development of MacNeice's poetry away from the brilliant surfaces of his earlier years towards the dark parable-like utterances of his last three books, which display a moral and philosophical concern to find meaning in life that his father would surely have approved. 'The Truisms' is a quest poem, evoking an allegorical journey that returns to the place it began — his father's home. The tone is tense, possibly even rueful, (which note I think Mr. Moore has mistaken for satire), but concludes with what in MacNeice's world must be a celebration, for images of growth for this poet are almost always positive:

> And he walked straight in; it was where he had come from
> And something told him the way to behave.
> He raised his hand and blessed his home;
> The truisms flew and perched on his shoulders
> And a tall tree sprouted from his father's grave.

The home which 'Happy Families' scornfully rejected, is now his own, is a locus of values which could help sustain a life.

What were the values that MacNeice came to feel his father's world represented and which he increasingly respected? Firstly, I would suggest it represented the possibility of belonging. MacNeice knew his father belonged to Ireland. He himself realized, as many of his late poems record, that he did not fully belong anywhere. Instead of a horizon which understood him he admitted,

> Now through the swinging doors of the decades I
> Confront a waste of tarmac, a roaring sky;
> The Southern Cross supplants the Useful Plough. . . .
> > ('Half Truth from Cape Town')

and reflected sadly in 'Restaurant Car'

> We roughride over the sleepers, finger the menu,
> Avoid our neighbours' eyes and wonder what

> Mad country moves beyond the steamed-up window. . . .

When he was younger such cultural dislocation had not mattered so profoundly — the city, despite the threat of war, political terror and loneliness was

> beauty narcotic and deciduous
> In this vast organism grown out of us:
> On all the traffic-islands stand white globes like moons,
> The city's haze is clouded amber that purrs and croons,
> And tilting by the noble curve bus after tall bus comes
> With an osculation of yellow light, with a glory like
> chrysanthemums.
>
> ('An Eclogue for Christmas')

The metropolis, rootless and threatened as life was there, offered compensations. In middle age, however, the city became for Mac-Neice 'One waste of traffic jams, one jam of dearth' ('Autumn Sequel'), 'the great mean city', where nobody belonged in the drab society that emerged in post-war London:

> From which reborn into anticlimax
> We endured much litter and apathy hoping
> The phoenix would rise, for so they had promised.
> Nevertheless let the petals fall
> Fast from the flower of cities all.

> And nobody rose, only some meaningless
> Buildings and the people once more were strangers
> At home with no one, sibling or friend.
> Which is why now the petals fall
> Fast from the flower of cities all.
>
> ('Goodbye to London')

In his father MacNeice had an image of an integration between life and place that he increasingly came to feel deprived of. His father also, I would argue, provided the poet with an example of the integration between belief and action that he as a writer sought through most of his life, though for him as poet, this ideal was expressed as a desire to integrate idea and poem, belief and art. In 1932, as a young man MacNeice had confessed an ambition 'to make an exhaustive study of seventeenth-century English prose (e.g. Donne, Jeremy Taylor, Sir T. Browne, Milton, etc.) and show how its cadences and imagery are a better union with God than any

English prose before or since. . . .' This interest and respect for style and content, belief and action in synthesis remained with him throughout his life. It was one of the things he most admired about his father 'whose life / Presumed the Resurrection' and belief in which 'made him courteous / And lyrical and strong and kind and truthful.' So MacNeice wrote of his father in *The Strings are False*:

> . . . greatly though he now exasperated me, I would remember how my father would come in to breakfast on Easter Day beaming as though he had just received a legacy; and I realized that his life, though not by any stretch of imagination a life for me, was more all of a piece, more purposeful, more satisfying to himself and perhaps to others than the lives of most people I knew.

He sought a similar integration in his poetry. In his study *Modern Poetry: a Personal Essay* (1938), Mac Neice asserted: 'The good poet has a definite attitude to life; most good poets, I fancy, have beliefs. . . .' He returns to discuss the relationship of belief and poetry in his study *The Poetry of W. B. Yeats* (1941), concerned to understand how Yeats's beliefs were related to his art, depending there on a notion of a coherence between the poet's personality and his beliefs, similar to that expressed in the lines on his father in 'The Kingdom':

> Poetry gains body from belief and the more suited the belief is to the poet, the healthier his poetry; one poet can thrive on pantheism and another on Christianity.

The poets whom MacNeice most admired as he grew older were those in whom he felt belief and style seemed most integrated, Spenser and Herbert. In *Varieties of Parable* (the Clark lectures which he delivered at Cambridge in the last year of his life) he returned again to worry the problem of how beliefs function in literature, concerned that 'in the twentieth century . . . realism in the photographic sense is almost played out and no longer satisfies our need', arguing that belief is needed in literature to play 'a part in the shaping of the poem. Which means that in this respect the beliefs are formalising elements.' Statements which John Frederick MacNeice would have found unexceptionable if applied to life. It does not seem to me unduly fanciful to suggest that MacNeice's formulation of his position in this way may well derive from the respect he felt for his father and his father's world as well as for the poetry of Spenser and Herbert. The formulations are those of a man who has felt the force of the Puritan vision — for life and art formalised by the discipline of belief is a Puritan ideal. Many of MacNeice's late poems, austere, tautly wrought parables permeated with emotional energy deriving from moral categories as many of them are, certainly are the poems of a mind that has felt the potency of the Puritan view of life. A poem such as 'The Slow Starter' (1960) is a long way from those astonishing, brilliant, early poems in which MacNeice celebrated 'the drunkenness of things being various' or 'the dazzle on the sea'. It is closer in tone and mood to his father's world of responsibility, commitment, judgment and possible punishment, that world he could never fully leave behind:

> O never force the pace, they said;
> Leave it alone, you have lots of time,
> Your kind of work is none the worse
> For slow maturing. Do not rush.
>> He took their tip, he took his time,
>> And found his time and talent gone.
>
> Oh you have had your chance, It said;
> Left it alone and it was one.
> Who said a watched clock never moves?
> Look at it now. Your chance was I.
>> He turned and saw the accusing clock
>> Race like a torrent round a rock.

LOUIS MAC NEICE
AT BIRMINGHAM

E. R. DODDS

Like most of the things I have valued in my life, my friendship with Louis MacNeice came about by sheer chance. In the summer of 1930, when I was Professor of Greek at Birmingham University, I advertised for an assistant lecturer. Among the applicants was an undergraduate of Merton College, Oxford, who had just taken his final examination — with what result was not yet known. The College authorities said this young man was unusually gifted but unfortunately rather a difficult character — he spent too much time writing poetry. The description attracted me: Birmingham was short of poets, and I had been a difficult character at Oxford myself. So I summoned him for interview, liked him at sight, and persuaded the University to appoint him. We worked together for the next six years, until 1936 when I returned to Oxford and he moved to Bedford College, London.

Louis was just twenty-three when he came to Birmingham. Father D'Arcy wrote to me from Oxford that Providence had committed to my care a very rare and exceptional person and that I must accept my responsibility. I doubt if I did for Louis all that Providence and Father D'Arcy would have wished, but I found my responsibility congenial. He was an enchanting companion — gay, mercurial, sometimes fantastic, but always with an underlying sobriety of judgement and a hint of underlying melancholy. His reaction to any experience was unpredictable, being entirely his own; it gave his talk a freshness that in our stale society we very seldom encountered. I had the feeling of great unused reserves, potentialities that he did not yet know how to develop.

From his schooldays onwards Louis had been influenced by the aestheticism that was fashionable in the nineteen-twenties: things (he had been taught to believe) were more interesting than people; art was more interesting than life; and in art all that mattered was Significant Form — its content was quite unimportant. At Oxford he had been a somewhat lonely aesthete: he had not shared the usual undergraduate interests and had taken little trouble to know his fellow-students, outside a very small circle of intimate friends. Birmingham was his first introduction to the ordinary world; it humanised his aestheticism and set free his natural love of life, but the process took some time. He was faced simultaneously with two new experiences — marriage and earning his living.

He had married immediately on leaving Oxford and had brought his young wife Mary to live in a converted stable where they played an endless innocent game of 'keeping house' like a pair of grown-up children: more like children, perhaps, than was altogether wholesome on a long-term view. His wife saw the stable as an Enchanted Island where the two of them would live happy ever after, decorating it and buying toys for it and keeping dogs and pigeons, with the vulgar commercial city and its tiresome university firmly shut out. In this domestic charade Louis played his part willingly enough: he would always throw himself with gusto into any game of make-believe. In these first years he seldom ventured outside the Island save in company with his wife. It was only later, when she was occupied with her baby and the make-believe was wearing a little thin, that he began to go about freely and discover new friends, like Ernst Stahl and John Waterhouse among his colleagues, Reggie Smith and Henry Reed among the students.

All through these formative years Louis was quietly teaching himself to write. Besides a book on Roman Humour which he never quite finished, he composed a fantastic play, *Station Bell*, which was acted by the Birmingham students and a too simple-minded novel. These juvenile experiments were balanced by a real achievement, his splendid verse translation of the *Agamemnon*: the present Professor of Greek at Oxford, Hugh Lloyd-Jones, told me not long ago that he thinks it the most successful version of any Greek tragedy that any one in this country has yet produced. At the same time Louis was labouring to perfect his skill as a lyric poet. As an undergraduate he had produced a slim volume called *Blind Fireworks*, but it showed only occasional promise of what was to come. The characteristic flux of images was there, but it was uncontrolled and lacked purpose; as he said himself, he 'just let the poem happen'. From childhood he had always been fascinated by words, which for him had an independent life of their own: as he put it in an unpublished early poem, 'I watched the words Coming to drink at my mind.' His problem was to capture and tame the words

before they flew away. During his years at Birmingham he wrote
many lyrics that he did not publish; he was slowly transforming
himself by hard work into the master craftsman that he had it in
him to be. His best poems of this period are all written in tightly
controlled forms — and indeed I think this is true of the majority
of his successful poems of all periods. Free verse did not really suit
him: in order to control the flux, he needed the discipline of a set
form, preferably a rhyming form.

I would add that for Louis the flux was not only an aesthetic
problem; it was also, in another of its aspects, a metaphysical
problem which disturbed him deeply. He was a man who by his
own confession adored the surfaces of things; but the surfaces would
not stay put. In his autobiography he remarks that what makes life
worth living for him is the surrender to certain moments — 'it may
be,' he says, 'to the life-quickening urge of an air raid, to nonsense
talked by one's friends, to a girl on top of the Empire State
building, to the silence of a ruined Byzantine church, to music,
drink, or the smell of turf smoke, to the first view of the Atlantic
or to the curve of a strand that seems to stretch to nowhere or
everywhere.' But such moments are fatally impermanent, and his
poems are haunted from first to last by the melancholy of their
transience. Louis was for ever trying to clutch 'a fringe or two of
the windy past'. There were rare instants when — for an instant —
he felt he had succeeded:

> Time was away and somewhere else,
> There were two glasses and two chairs
> And two people with the one pulse
> (Somebody stopped the moving stairs):
> Time was away and somewhere else,
>
> ('Meeting Point')

But always the stairs would move again; time would return, and the
melancholy with it.

In this world of shifting appearances Louis had nothing to hold
on to — except himself. He would enslave his judgement and his
conscience to no '-ism', religious or political. This does *not* mean
that he was indifferent. He rejected Christianity with consistent
firmness, but the questions that troubled him all his life were at
bottom religious questions. He subscribed to no Party programme,
but he shared to the full the political anxieties of our time. He held

that a poet's duty to his society was neither greater nor less than the ordinary citizen's. It carried with it no obligation to political or religious commitment, but it did carry a need for concern. He was no cynical bystander. There were a few things he was sure of. He was once challenged to state publicly what he believed. He replied: 'I believe that life is worth while, and I believe that I have to do something *for* life. I believe that as a human being it is my duty to make patterns and to contribute to order — good patterns and a good order.' To this simple creed he remained true. Louis was a good pattern-maker, and through his patterns he made, as it seems to me, a lasting contribution to a good order.

'A FANCY TURN, YOU KNOW'

BERNARD SHARE

The beard suited him. In the photograph facing page 225 of *Letters from Iceland* he looks like a leprechaun discovered popping one more piece of gold into his crock. But if he vomited noisily in the white Icelandic summer night he was winning at cards and perhaps at other things: 'The luck,' Auden tells us, 'is all MacNeice's.' He arrived late — W.H.A. had already done most of the homework — and never, except for the purposes of rhetoric, tried to make out that the experience was anything more than a phrase between square brackets: 'Holidays should be like this, / Free from over-emphasis.' This was nothing like Spain, to be remembered so evocatively in *Autumn Journal*, but 'a fancy turn, you know, / Sandwiched in a graver show'. Auden, though at times taking himself and his experiences a good deal more seriously, caught the mood. The most serious things in *Letters from Iceland* were written by other people, most of them, even then, dead.

> Not only have individuals, of purely scientific habits, had their curiosity awakened and gratified by the details of natural research, with which they have been presented by those who have recently visited Iceland, with a view to explore its extraordinary phenomena; but such as bend their attention more to the history of man, and especially those who wish to contemplate him as affected by the influence of moral and religious principle, have felt a most lively concern about the inhabitants of that remote country, and expressed an ardent desire of becoming more intimately acquainted with the peculiarities of their character and habits of life.

Thus Ebenezer Henderson, for whom Iceland in 1814 offered both a challenge (he was a religious propagandist) and a stimulus. Half a century or so later, Lord Dufferin found that Reykjavik contained no more than 700 or 800 inhabitants. And in 1936, it is well to remember, Iceland was still what is now an incredible four-and-a-half days away and very little changed, if one excepts the advent of the internal combustion engine, from the days of the Sagas. Even as late as 1960 there was only one place in the country where you could legally consume strong drink. Not surprising, therefore, that the section 'For Tourists' in the *Letters* should read like a Victorian safari guide, even down to the language: 'Everyone has their medicines, but from personal experience I would recommend chlorodyne as the best stuff to take in cases of internal disorder.' Iceland was, and remained until the arrival of the Americans and the aeroplane, a low-temperature Tahiti, a kind of Puritan paradise, an image of a society admired — from a safe distance — for its exotically plain virtues. It existed, in the mind of the urban Englishman, not of itself but by contrast; and Auden, throughout the *Letters*, continually points this up. MacNeice, for his part, could afford to be somewhat more detached ('Wystan said that he was planning to go / To Iceland to write a book and would I come too; / And I said yes, having nothing better to do.' And, of course, being Irish, he had seen something like this before. Much of the country resembles a totally treeless Connemara; the domestic architecture, though executed in corrugated iron, has a familiar ring to it and in any case the Irish had got there first: ('Old Irish hermits, holy skin and bone, camped on these crags in order to forget / Their blue-black cows in Kerry pastures wet.') The forced, flat rhyme is symptomatic: MacNeice, in this 'Letter to Graham and Anne Shepard', is determined not to be impressed—or perhaps just unable. In contrast with the romantic engravings illustrating Henderson and Dufferin the landscape seems deflated and featureless — too much of a muchness. The colours are as subtle — and as immediately unappealing — as the Australian drab green. Auden was clearly doing his best to turn it into a country of the mind — and anyway he had undertaken to write the book. MacNeice could ask himself quite candidly '. . . Qu'allais-je faire / Among these volcanic rocks and this grey air?'

What he did is what people did — and do — in Iceland if they came as tourists: ride around on horses feeling uncomfortable and virtuous, battle with the worst cooking in Europe, try to sleep through the overlit nights and daydream of dim, decadent bars. 'We . . . Have minds no match / For this land's girth', wrote MacNeice in the one poem ('Iceland') in which he really tried to assess the nature of the place. Much of the rest of his contribution is almost waywardly backward-looking, culminating in the garrulous

'Auden and MacNeice: Their Last Will and Testament' which laboriously catalogued the foibles of their London friends and could have been written without leaving St. John's Wood.

Between the lines he was, of course, enjoying himself, recognising that this was a real escape from the personal problems then besetting him — a therapeutic interlude. The experience, however, was absorbed, the influences, such as they were, failed to make themselves evident in any substantive form in the later work. A brief visit like this, with someone else's thumb in the guidebook, could scarcely have resulted otherwise. But if Iceland the country failed to materialise as a creative locus in its own right, the literature was another matter. A literature very much part of its landscape: it would be difficult not to assume that the Sagas said more to MacNeice after his acquaintanceship with their physical setting. Not that, even here, there is much to go on: the *persona* of the Troll, in a couple of wartime poems; three radio adaptations and a pair of 'Dark Age Glosses' in *Solstices* (1961). Here, the echoes are very faint, and the gloss on the Four Masters, with its Irish setting, is by far the most vivid and realised of the set.

The *terminus ad quem* itself, the book *Letters from Iceland*, is a curiously self-divided production. Faber's designer, Richard de la Mare, did it proud. Fashions in typography change almost as rapidly as those in hemlines, but the currently unpopular Bodoni, so much a part of the Faber image of the era, was skilfully deployed to try to effect an amalgam between the diverse and divergent elements. The illustrations are interesting but uneven, the factual material comprehensive if idiosyncratic. The 'literary' element is perhaps the weakest: some of the verse is little better than doggerel — jokey, awkward, almost perversely non-poetic — and MacNeice's one attempt at a more concentrated and finished lyric, whilst pleasing enough, reads as if written to order.

A non-book, then, the fruit of a non-event? Scarcely. As an unconventional compendium *Letters from Iceland* is a distinct advance on the run-of-the-mill travel book, and its high spirits and irreverent sense of discovery and self-discovery are infectious. It is clear enough, however, that MacNeice, in spite of the political props of 'Eclogue from Iceland', was not taking anything very seriously. 'No ghost was scotched', as he says in the 'Epilogue', and there was 'Time for soul to stretch and spit / Before the world comes back on it.' The returning world was to bring *Autumn Journal* and much more — good use had been made of a re-fuelling stop. As the Icelandic proverb has it: 'The haddock never wanders wide, but it has the same spot by its side.' Whatever that may mean.

CELT AND CLASSICIST:
THE VERSECRAFT OF
LOUIS MACNEICE

ROBIN SKELTON

Louis MacNeice was trained as a classical scholar, and from his prep school days onward was obliged to spend a good deal of time in the scansion of classical metres. In his unfinished autobiography he says that his classical teacher at Sherborne 'was the first who thrilled me by reading poetry' and tells how, in teaching the pupils to scan Latin hexametres, 'he would stride up and down the room slowly, yards to each stride, intoning "Spon-dee! Spon-dee!" Spon upon the left foot and Dee upon the right.' In his senior year at Marlborough his classical teacher 'concentrated with gusto on grammar and syntax'. It is not, therefore, particularly surprising to discover that at Oxford 'style remained more important than subject' to him. His interest in style and in prosody persisted. In 1941 he told L.A.G. Strong in a BBC discussion, 'Well, I have read a good deal about the theory of metre and I do know how to analyse the various traditional metrical forms, and actually I do know how to practise them if I want to.' Nevertheless he felt that, 'the point of having rules is that you can break them. The artist needs a limit within which to work and he needs a norm from which to deviate.' MacNeice deviated from the 'norm' with real brilliance. William T. McKinnon in his study of the poet (*Apollo's Blended Dream*, London, 1971) describes his variations as resulting from an 'interplay of intuited rhythm and regular metrical pattern' and gives some interesting examples of the way in which MacNeice brought new vitality to an established verse-medium or form by utilizing skilful substitution and by deploying elaborate patterns of near-rhyme, assonance and consonance. That MacNeice was a master practitioner of orthodox metrics hardly needs to be proved. We can point to the regular Ballades of 1940, the octosyllabic couplets of 'Child's Unhappiness', and the *terza rima* of *Autumn Sequel*, and numerous other poems whose deviations from the norm would be totally acceptable to disciples of Saintsbury. What does perhaps need to be examined anew is the way in which he developed methods of verse-construction which have little to do with the schemae of classical prosody, and yet which, when applied to classical structures, provide the verse with a new bite and brilliance.

It is necessary here to digress a little. McKinnon, and most other writers concerned, if only briefly, with English prosody tend to assume that rhythmical verse must necessarily be based upon metrical structures familiar to students of the classics, and that any variations they exhibit are likely to be, (to use McKinnon's word), 'intuitive'. This may be true in the majority of cases. When one is tackling the work of a Celt, however, one must remember that the Welsh and the Irish utilized devices and structures that only a minority of the English even now understand. It is true that one can detect in the English poetry of the sixteenth and seventeenth centuries a good many forms which appear to derive from the simpler of the twenty-four official Welsh metres. Herrick has examples of a number of these. It is also true that the octosyllabic rhyming couplet was familiar to Welsh poets long before it became a feature of French poetry, whence (it is usually supposed) it came into use in England. If one were to attempt to list the ways in which Welsh and Irish practice differ from English (which means, I suppose, Anglo-French, Anglo-Italian, and Neo-Classical) practice, at least after the beginning of the fifteenth century, one would have to make a number of basic points. Firstly, although there are many Welsh and Irish metres which use lines with an even number of syllables, (the Welsh being particularly addicted to four-syllable and eight-syllable lines), there are quite as many which employ lines of three, five, seven and nine syllables. Lines of this length rarely occur regularly in English verse, perhaps because of the dominance of the iambic and trochaic tradition. Secondly, in both Welsh and Irish verse, more attention is paid to patterns of assonance, consonance, and alliteration than in English verse. Indeed, there are established patterns upon which the verse is based rather than upon stress patterns. Moreover, in both Welsh and Irish verse it is not infrequently laid down that certain words which are crucial to the structure should possess a defined number of syllables. Thus, in the Irish *Rannaigecht Gairit*, a quatrain rhyming abab, the end words of the first and third lines are monosyllables and the end words of the second and fourth lines are disyllables, the end word of the third line also rhyming with a word in the middle of the fourth line. The first line has three syllables and the remainder have seven. Moreover, in some Irish and Welsh forms, it is clearly specified that certain rhymes should be 'near rhymes' and not masculine ones. Indeed, the Welsh *Cywydd deuair hirion* and the Irish *Deibide* are both composed in seven syllable couplets which rhyme a stressed with an unstressed syllable, and the *Englyn proest dalgron* is composed in stanzas of four seven-syllable lines all linked by an assonantal form of near-rhyme; no masculine rhyme is permitted.

Louis MacNeice, though he spent a great deal of his life in England, was an Irishman. He described himself in *I Crossed the Minch* as

> descended from an Irish king — the name MacNeice being derived from Conchubar MacNessa, the villain of the Deirdre saga. (In later years I was told that the derivation was much more probably from Naiose, the hero of the same saga, and since then I have, in defiance of natural history, claimed descent from both of them and in each case by Deirdre.

MacNeice was very conscious of his Irishry, especially as a boy and young man, and while he did not know Gaelic, it is unlikely that one so sensitive to speech-tunes and so interested in metrics, would not have picked up something of Irish verse in his many visits to the West. Moreover, he was sufficiently interested in Irish poetry to write a book on W. B. Yeats, and in his book on modern poetry he suggested that one way to avoid giving the impression of artificiality in formally structured verse was to use 'internal rhymes, off-rhymes, bad rhymes, "para-rhymes" '; he also suggested that one might rhyme stressed with unstressed syllables. In this he may not have been doing more than commend methods he had arrived at 'intuitively'; it is, however, not unlikely that his intuition had been assisted by his memories of Irish speech and by his reading of Irish and Welsh literature.

There is no doubt that a number of his poems had their beginnings in technical experimentation. He once told me that he sometimes selected a form and then worked within it until lines began to be 'given', finding that the form and metre occupied his conscious mind and allowed intuition full play, even that a metre could 'hypnotise' him and permit inspiration to occur. Certainly when one looks at some of his poems it is clear that, while some variations may be chance, many are deliberate. 'Aubade' of 1934 shows him approximating to the *Deibide* already mentioned, though the line has been lengthened from seven to eleven syllables (to take the average, for the syllable count is 11, 10, 11, 11, 12, 12). In the couplet the lines are linked by assonance (*apple/happy*), in the second by true *Deibide* rhyme (*blue/to*), and in the third by assonance (*dawn/war*). Moreover, in the first two couplets, which are dominated by lyrical recollection, we find both alliteration and a touch of that echoing of the final syllables of one line in the first syllables of the next which is part of the formula for *Englyn penfyr* (*apple/Or, pl* . . .). Moreover, in the middle of all the first four lines we find an 'f' sound which is made prominent by its being accompanied by a number of 'fs' and 'vs' (v being, after all, a voiced f) surrounding it. The last two lines have a hard 'g' as the central consonant. These features may, just possibly, have been created 'intuitively', but they certainly form a quite precise pattern.

AUBADE

Having bitten on life like a sharp apple
Or, playing it like a fish, been happy,

Having felt with fingers that the sky is blue,
What have we after that to look forward to?

Not the twilight of the gods but a precise dawn
Of sallow and grey bricks, and newsboys crying war.

A search through MacNeice's verse reveals that, at one point or another, he has used almost all the rhyming and near-rhyming devices of Welsh and Irish poetry. *Aicill* (or internal) rhyme is frequent, and lines are frequently linked by consonance as in many traditional Irish and Welsh metres. Thus the first verse of 'Order to View' (March 1940) reads:

It was a big house, bleak;
Grass on the drive;
We had been there before
But memory, weak in front of
A blistered door, could find
Nothing alive now;

> The shrubbery dripped, a crypt
> Of leafmould dreams; a tarnished
> Arrow over an empty stable
> Shifted a little in the tenuous wind.

The end words of the first three lines have *aicill* rhyme with lines four, five and six. The last consonant of line seven reappears in the penultimate word of line nine, and the last word of line eight is in consonance with the penultimate word of line ten.

The second stanza follows a different scheme, being structured around the repetition of a small number of consonants and vowel sounds. The words thus connected are: *unable, wall, loose, loops, bubble, faltered, dull, bell-pull, pull, ill, world* (all using 'l'), *rise, trees, loose, loops, rose, use, place, supposed, closed* (all using sibillants), and *wishes, were wall, one, wish, what, one, was, world* (the 'w' sound). There are other links. 'Loose' rhymes, *aicill* fashion, with 'loops', 'pull' with 'whole', and 'supposed' with 'closed', and the word 'pull' appears twice in one line.

> And wishes were unable
> To rise; on the garden wall
> The pear trees had come loose
> From rotten loops; one wish,
> A rainbow bubble, rose,
> Faltered, broke in the dull
> Air — What was the use?
> The bell-pull would not pull
> And the whole place, one might
> Have supposed, was deadly ill:
> The world was closed.

The third stanza is similarly dominated by patterns of repeating consonants and vowels.

Neither of the two poems we have glanced at are metrically regular, and it may therefore be suspected that MacNeice rarely utilized the same pattern in successive stanzas. The lie to this can be given by glancing at the extraordinarily deft and precise construction of 'The Sunlight on the Garden'. In each stanza the pattern is the same, with only tiny variants. Line one is of seven syllables, and is in catalectic iambic tetrameter; line two varies in length from five to seven syllables but is made up of a choriamb,

and one to three additional syllables, one of which is always stressed
and concludes the line; line three is, again, a seven syllable catalectic iambic tetrameter; line four is of six syllables and is iambic tri-
meter with trochaic substitution in the first foot; line five is regular
iambic dimeter, and line six is of seven syllables each time (if we
read 'we are' as approximating to 'we're' as the cadence demands
and as MacNeice himself read it), and is catalectic iambic tetrameter, with trochaic substitution in the second foot of the last line,
as in the first line of the whole poem.

This regularity of form is also revealed in the verbal repetitions.
The poem begins and ends with what is, to all intent, the same line.
Similarly the middle two stanzas each contain the words 'The earth
compels'. In all stanzas the end word of the first line rhymes di-
syllabically with the first word of the second, and the last word of
the third line and the first of the fourth are similarly connected.
The end-rhyme scheme in each stanza is abcbba. The a rhyme is
disyllabic and the b is monosyllabic. The poem utilizes internal
consonance and assonance to good effect, and a small group of
words are repeated several times during the poem, sometimes within
the lines (*Epanorthosis*) and sometimes at the beginning of them
(*Epanaphora*). These patterns are so organized as to give the poem
musical coherence and progression. Thus in the first stanza four of
the six lines begin with the sound 'w'. In each of the next two
stanzas one line begins with the word 'We'; in the final stanza the
'w' sound appears only once and unobtrusively in the word 'anew'.
This pattern is reversed in the handling of the word 'and'. In
stanza one, as in all the stanzas, it appears in the middle of one
line. It first appears as the opening word of a line in the second
stanza; it also begins one line of the third stanza. The final stanza
uses it twice as the beginning of a line.

Other patterns emerge as soon as one begins to look for them.
The first two lines of each stanza are linked by similar vowel and
consonants being used in the first foot of the line, these being 'n'
in stanza one, 'f' (voiced as 'v') in stanza two, 'y' in stanza three,
and 'd' and 'n' in stanza four. A consonant in the first foot of the
last line of stanzas one, three and four reappears in the last foot of
the line; in stanza two a vowel sound is repeated. This pattern of
repeated sounds is given a climactic emphasis in the last stanza by
consonantal links between the first foot of the third and the fifth
line, (But *glad*/*And grate-*), and the first foot of the fourth and
sixth (*Thund-*/*For sun-*). There are other, less regularly patterned,

instances of alliteration, consonance, and assonance in other parts of the poem.

When 'The Sunlight on the Garden' is read from this structural point of view it reveals a subtlety, strength, and cunning which places it as one of the most impressive lyrical constructions of the century.

THE SUNLIGHT ON THE GARDEN

The sunlight on the garden
Hardens and grows cold,
We cannot cage the minute
Within its nets of gold,
When all is told
We cannot beg for pardon.

Our freedom as free lances
Advances towards its end;
The earth compels, upon it
Sonnets and birds descend;
And soon, my friend,
We shall have no time for dances.

The sky was good for flying
Defying the church bells
And every evil iron
Siren and what it tells:
The earth compels,
We are dying, Egypt, dying

And not expecting pardon,
Hardened in heart anew,
But glad to have sat under
Thunder and rain with you,
And grateful too
For sunlight on the garden.

Most of MacNeice's regularly formed lyrics reveal the same group of technical devices. The 'Finale' of the sequence from *Out of the Picture* is another instance of the expert handling of Celtic devices.

The last word of the first line is linked by consonance to the first four of the second, and all the lines have internal consonance. The last stanza (in which the devices are used most obviously) may serve as an example

> A kiss, a cuddle,
> A crossed cheque,
> *The trimmed wick burns clear,*
> Walk among statues in the dark,
> The odds are you will break your neck —
> *Here ends our hoarded oil.*

MacNeice is fond of *Epanorthosis*. In 'London Rain' he uses it at the end of lines four and six of each stanza, making it appear to be *rime riche,* though in fact only in one stanza (stanza three) does the second appearance of the word carry a meaning different from the first and thus present the true *rime riche* phenomenon. In this poem he also uses locution patterns and parallelism, repeating a syntactical construction in adjacent lines, as in

> The randy mares of fancy
> The stallions of the soul

and

> The world is what was given,
> The world is what we make.

Although the rhymes scheme of each stanza could be described as abcbdb, two of the a, c and d lines are usually linked either by consonance or assonance, and the third is only similar to the others in being a trochaic disyllable. Thus in stanza one we have the a, c and d words, *pimples/London/jungle.* In stanzas two and three they are *violent/fancy/fences* and *chimneys/channel/No-God,* the last being (exceptionally) a spondee. The pattern is varied in only two of the remaining eight stanzas. Again, there is much internal consonance and assonance throughout. The first stanza may serve as an illustration.

> The rain of London pimples
> The ebony street with white
> And the neon-lamps of London
> Stain the canals of night
> And the park becomes a jungle
> In the alchemy of night.

All these poems are orthdox and regular metrically. Sometimes,
however, MacNeice abandons metre altogether and structures his
work entirely upon the kind of patterning I have been describing.
When he does this he relies heavily upon locution patterns and
parallelism, *Epanaphora* and *Spanorthosis*. A good example is, of
course, 'Prayer Before Birth'. The fifth verse paragraph runs:

> I am not yet born; rehearse me
> In the parts I must play and the cues I must take when
> old men lecture me, bureaucrats hector me, mountains
> frown at me, lovers laugh at me, the white
> waves call me to folly and the desert calls
> me to doom and the beggar refuses
> my gift and my children curse me.

It does not require much acuteness of observation to see the internal
rhyming, the consonance, the assonance, and the parallelism. The
whole poem is, of course, built up on incantatory repetition. Other
obvious instances of this are 'Visitations' I and VI, 'Bagpipe Music'
(which, however, is obtrusively and deftly metrical), 'Jericho',
'Invocation', and, of course, 'Château Jackson' which is based
upon 'The House that Jack Built', but improves the original with
many internal rhymes and consonantal patterns. The first part of
the poem runs:

> Where is the Jack that built the house
> That housed the folk that tilled the field
> That filled the bags that brimmed the mill
> That ground the flour that browned the bread
> That fed the serfs that scrubbed the floors
> That wore the mats that kissed the feet
> That bore the bums that raised the heads
> That raised the eyes that eyed the glass
> That sold the pass that linked the lands
> That sink the sands that told the time
> That stopped the clock that guards the shelf
> That shrines the frame that lacks the face
> That mocked the man that sired the Jack
> That chanced the arm that bought the farm
> That caught the wind that skinned the flocks

That raised the rocks that sunk the ship
That rode the tide that washed the bank
That grew the flowers that brewed the red
That stained the page that drowned the loan
That built the house that Jack built?

The sheer dexterity and brilliance of this poem, and its air of spontaneity, should not blind us to the tight patterns of its structure, any more than the ease and masterly poise of *Autumn Journal* should prevent us from noticing the extraordinary richness of its music and the way in which almost every known device of verse-craft is brought in to support and control the structure. In the twenty-fourth section, for example, we find a strong and effective use of *Epanaphora* and consonance.

Sleep, my fancies and my wishes,
    Sleep a little and wake strong,
The same but different and take my blessing —
    A cradle-song.
And sleep, my various and conflicting
    Selves I have so long endured,
Sleep in Asclepius' temple
    And wake cured.

In other parts of the poem we find the incidental use of internal rhyme, and are dazzled by the cunning of such lines as

Still alive even if forbidden, hidden

in which every word in the line chimes with another one, and

Come over, they said, into Macedonia and help us

in which what appears to be a laconic rather workaday statement is given strength by the way in which the main consonants and vowels of the first half of the line are repeated in the second half of the same line in the same order, (*Come*/*Mac, over*/*onia, said*/ *help*). This particular device, which in Welsh would be regarded as a form of *Cynghanedd*, is not infrequent in MacNeice's longer and more discursive poems, though it is never permitted to obtrude except when it is used to point up a joke or contribute to helter-skelter levity. It is indeed, often unnoticeable, art concealing art, as perhaps in the lines

> We wrote compositions in Greek which they said was a lesson
> In logic and good for the brain

in which a hard 'c' is followed by a hard 'g' in each line, and the last foot of the first line is linked to the first of the second by consonance in 'l'.

It may be, as McKinnon suggests, that MacNeice contrived these effects intuitively rather than with full awareness of what he was doing, but it seems unlikely. There are many effects which might have been the result of simply seeking a musical language, but there are many others which are so schematically organized as to make accident improbable. Clearly, either MacNeice managed to arrive at the same conclusions about verse structure as the early Welsh and Irish poets, or he deliberately studied and learned from them. It is true, of course, that the Welsh and Irish poets were not alone in employing the devices I have uncovered; many of them can also be found in the Classical Literature of which MacNeice was a scholar. Nevertheless, I am persuaded that MacNeice, conscious and proud of his Irish ancestry from an early age, and a man clearly and admittedly fascinated by technique, could not but have dipped into Celtic prosody. He found there principles of structure which he then used both together with, and apart from the classical metres he knew so well, and brought to English verse a dexterous verbal music which has received much less attention than the more obvious, and sometimes ostentatious, 'mouth music' of his friend Dylan Thomas, who, though not a Welsh speaker, also clearly learned from traditional Welsh forms. MacNeice, indeed, in his versecraft, brought together the English and the Celtic traditions, as also did Yeats in some of his later poems. He was, however, stylistically a more various poet than Yeats; he was, indeed, in his enthusiasm for technique, closer to the multi-skilled Pound who also brought into English verse devices and effects learned from other tongues and centuries. Now, eleven years after his death, it is high time for Louis MacNeice to be recognized as one of the master craftsmen in our poetry, and for his poems to be established as essential reading for any who care to study or to practise the intricacies of English verse.

MAC NEICE AS CRITIC

WALTER ALLEN

It is doubtful whether MacNeice thought of himself as a literary critic or took criticism itself very seriously. In *Modern Poetry* he wrote: 'Writing about poetry often becomes a parlour game. The critic is more interested in producing a water-tight system of criticism than in the objects which are his data.' The temper of his mind was essentially sceptical and vigorously independent; and he was suspicious of systems and system-making. But he was widely and deeply read in poetry and had a more than casual acquaintance with philosophy and psychology and an informed interest in the goings-on of the world generally. Above all, he was a learned practitioner of his craft. All this, it seems to me, gave him security as a poet; I do not think he ever doubted his taste or the basis of his taste. He was, more than most men, always himself; and when he came to writing about poetry he did so, as he says in *Modern Poetry*, 'as one who enjoys reading and writing certain (probably limited) kinds of poetry and is only concerned with criticism in so far as it clears away misapprehensions and opens the gate to poetry itself.'

He wrote a great deal of literary journalism and three critical books, *Modern Poetry* (1938), *The Poetry of W. B. Yeats* (1941), and *Varieties of Parable* (published posthumously in 1965), all of which are bound within the limits of his strongly idiosyncratic personality and are expressions of it. They are highly personal books. He says in *Modern Poetry*: 'Literary criticism should always be partly biographical', which he must have known would be regarded in many quarters as a heretical statement. In fact, his own criticism is always partly autobiographical: whatever he writes springs out of his own experience of poetry as reader and writer.

His lifelong taste in poetry, it seems to me, is stated in the first sentence of the preface to *Modern Poetry*: 'This book is a plea for *impure* poetry, that is, for poetry conditioned by the poet's life and the world around him.' Today, the main interest of *Modern Poetry* is probably of a period kind: it captures the sense of an age in poetry, the Thirties, and brings out what certain poets who emerged at the beginning of the decade were seeking to do as no other work of criticism does, and for this reason will obviously be permanently valuable. It is a kind of manifesto for a movement. It captures the mood of a time perfectly, as in poetry MacNeice captured perfectly the mood of a time in *Autumn Journal*. In a sense, it is a work of propaganda, as manifestos are, and no doubt the poetry of the period looks very different now from MacNeice's presentation of it. But it re-asserts some perennial truths about poetry, notably that stated by Synge, which is fundamental to the book: 'it is the timber of poetry that wears most surely, and there is no timber that has not strong roots among the clay and worms.' And reading *Modern Poetry* today, one is struck by the excellence of the technical criticism, which is a poet's and a poet's alone. I instance the following:

> But granting that a rhythmical basis, known or sensed, is an asset to a poem, I think that many poems (especially those which come from subtle or sophisticated subjects or moods) are the better for rhythmical variations, (a) because rhythmical variations can often be significant of variations in content, (b) because variety is delightful for its own sake. Mr. Young, intending a *reductio ad absurdum* of modern metric, brings up "Johnson's friend, who thought that if a line had ten syllables it was verse":

> > Put your knife and your fork across your plate.

> Now it is obvious that the rhythm of this line is not a rhythm fit to be repeated through all or most of the lines of a poem whose basis is taken to be the regular blank verse basis u — u — u — u — u — . But it is not obvious that such a line is unfit to enter such a poem at all. — u — u u — u — u — is a recognisable version of the blank verse line and as such may have its own emotional significance. For example, in a poem of melodrama describing an impending murder:

> > The dark is falling and the hour is late:
> > *Put your knife and your fork across your plate.*

> Here the change from the neat traditional rhythm of the first line to the halting rhythm of the second, which throws an

additional stress on "knife and fork", would to my ear have a sinister effect entirely in keeping with the subject. Broken rhythms have their uses, as have merely flat or pedestrian lines, or hiatus, which in itself is normally unpleasant; thus "the empty air" merely as sound is much emptier than "the vacant air".

Perhaps more than most poets, MacNeice, as his verse exemplifies, delighted in the dance of words and in the measures to which words can be persuaded to dance; and the expertise which he gained from his own practice as a poet is a constant strength of his criticism. And there is something else: MacNeice's scepticism of systems and the all-embracing generalisation. When writing of his growing appreciation of poetry at Marlborough, MacNeice remarks: 'Homer gave me an example of verse-writing which was homogeneous but yet elastic enough to represent much of life's variety. I have noticed since that many modern theories of poetry could not make room for Homer.' The comment is a reminder that, however novel MacNeice's theory and practice may have seemed thirty-five years ago, they related to the oldest traditions of poetry.

Besides this, besides being a work of propaganda, *Modern Poetry* is a 'missionary' work. MacNeice is his own guinea pig. He charts and illustrates the growth of his own pleasure in poetry from infancy and at the same time asserts the centrality of poetry to the life of man. He is able to do this because of the presentation of MacNeice himself.

My own prejudice, therefore, is in favour of poets whose worlds are not too esoteric. I would have a poet able-bodied, fond of talking, a reader of the newspapers, capable of pity and laughter, informed in economics, appreciative of women, involved in personal relationships, actively interested in politics, susceptible to physical impressions. The relationship between life and literature is almost impossible to analyse, but it should not be degraded into something like the translation of one language into another. For life is not literary, while literature is not, in spite of Plato, essentially second hand.

The combination of qualities — of learning, wit, professional expertise, seriousness that is never solemnity, enthusiasm — displayed in *Modern Poetry*, makes it, it seems to me, still an ideal introduction to its subject and indeed to poetry generally. And seen in this light, the fact that many of MacNeice's propositions are infinitely arguable makes it the more valuable.

The Poetry of W. B. Yeats may be seen as in some sense an appendage to *Modern Poetry*. It was the first study of Yeats to be published after the poet's death, the first of a whole string of critical studies. Professor K. G. W. Cross, in his survey of Yeats criticism in *In Excited Reverie*, a symposium published for the Yeats centenary in 1965 and edited by A. Norman Jeffares and Cross himself, comments: 'If Louis MacNeice's *The Poetry of W. B. Yeats* (1941) seems today rather thin and outmoded it can still be read for its perceptive comments on particular poems. Like W. H. Auden's essay 'Yeats as an Example' (in *The Permanence of Yeats*), its main interest lies in its reflection of what poets of the nineteen-thirties found to praise in Yeats.' The comment is fair. Inevitably, MacNeice's book has been overshadowed by later works by scholars like Ellman, Henn and Jeffares. Yet his book is not in competition with theirs and belongs to a very different kind of critical activity. It is valuable precisely because it is the response of one poet to another. Both were complex men, temperamentally utterly dissimilar. The one common factor was their Irishness, and this did not necessarily bridge the gulf between them. Writing in *Varieties of Parable*, MacNeice says: 'As a child I took among other things to Greek and Norse mythology. Curiously, since I lived in Ireland, I was not offered the early Irish legends but I doubt if I would have taken to them with equal enthusiasm.' He goes on: 'The pre-eminent Irish hero is Cuchulain; Yeats tried throughout his life to make something of him. But Cuchulain was unpromising material except—to the modern mind—for grotesque farce.' Then to MacNeice, Yeats's system of belief as laid down in *A Vision* could only have seemed mumbo-jumbo. He was bothered too by Yeats's fascist tendencies.

All the same, there is no question of his admiration for the elder poet. 'If I were making a general anthology of shorter English poems,' he begins his book by saying, 'I should want to include some sixty by W. B. Yeats. There is no other poet in the language from whom I should choose so many.' And it is plain that the reading of Yeats in bulk that went to the making of the book caused MacNeice to revise to some extent his view on poetry as expressed in *Modern Poetry*, in which, he said, 'I over-stressed the half-truth that poetry is *about* something, is Communication. So it is, but it is also a separate self; in the same way a living animal is an individual although it is on the one hand conditioned by the laws of heredity and environment and the laws of nature in general and on the other hand has a function outside itself, is a link in a chain.' It is worth remembering, I think, that though Yeats's reputation was great at the time of his death, it was not as great as it is today. MacNeice, who was no respecter of reputations, takes Yeats's greatness as a poet for granted. He pays Yeats the supreme compliment of seeing him with the same eye with which he saw his coevals.

The Poetry of W. B. Yeats seems to me, as I have said, in some sense an off-shoot of *Modern Poetry* and also a corrective to it, a continuation of the debate going on in MacNeice's mind on the nature of poetry. *Varieties of Parable,* the text of the Clark Lectures which he delivered at Cambridge a few months before his death, is different, an account and justification of his preferences in literature. MacNeice was in his fifties and a famous elder poet: the Thirties were long over. Perhaps the invitation from Cambridge to deliver the lectures came to him as an opportunity to sum up his tastes. We know from his unfinished autobiography *The Strings are False,* that in his boyhood *The Faerie Queene* was his favourite poem. Superficially, this may seem strange. Of the great English poets one suspects that Spenser appeals less to the modern mind than any other, but having said that, one recalls that centuries ago he was called the poet's poet, and certainly Spenser is at the root of MacNeice's argument. One regrets that he never devoted a whole book to Spenser.

In *Varieties of Parable* he writes: 'I would rather read Spenser than most. In poetry as a writer I have more often than not worked at the opposite pole to Spenser, confining myself largely (no poet can confine himself completely) to the external world and therefore at times becoming a journalist rather than a creative writer.' He goes on: 'Spenser, far from being a mere decorator or escapist or fantasist in the narrow sense, was a very serious writer, especially concerned with the realities of human life.' Part of his appeal for MacNeice lay in what he called his 'double-level writing' or 'sleight-of-hand writing'. MacNeice often expressed his distaste for realism or naturalism, and this despite the strong strain of realism in his poetry. To my knowledge, he nowhere deals with the novel, though he did publish one under a pseudonym, and reviewed them for a short time in the Thirties in *The Spectator*. What in effect he is doing in *Varieties of Parable*, it seems to me, is to put the case for romance in something like Northrop Frye's sense of the word.

He exemplifies it in the works of, among others, Spenser, Herbert, Bunyan, Kingsley, George MacDonald, Carroll, Kafka, Pinter, Beckett and Golding, writers who he admits are very disparate. But one can see they have a common quality: all are or can be construed as allegorists. All, too, are complex: they have to a greater or less degree what MacNeice finds in Spenser, 'exceptional depth and variety' and the 'richness and complexity of the best dreams and the truth to life of the best fairy stories.'

But MacNeice shuns the word 'romance' and, explaining why he eschews the words 'symbolism', 'fable', 'allegory', 'fantasy' and 'myth', plumps for the word 'parable', though he admits it is not entirely satisfactory. All the words he rejects can, he contends, 'be squeezed under the umbrella of "parable"'. Maybe; but it seems to me to make unnecessarily heavy weather of his running together of categories, and in fact it seems to me also that his terminology is too loose, partly, perhaps, because his enthusiasm for his scheme leads him to over-emphasize similarities between the works he deals with and prevents his seeing essential differences.

This in itself throws light up the kind of critical work *Varieties of Parable* is. A record of personal discoveries and personal preferences, it is related to the author's practice as a poet, particularly to his practice as a radio dramatist, where his theme, as in *The Dark Tower*, was so often the quest and the central character a version of Everyman. The text as we have it was not revised by the author, and indeed we do not know whether he himself would have published it. Certainly it captures wonderfully his speaking voice. It is full of critical perceptions on specific passages and its enthusiasm is delightful.

Its weakness, and in view of the subject it is a serious one, arises, it seems to me, from MacNeice's defective sympathies, in particular his aversion to the realistic novel. At times he seems unwilling to distinguish between newspaper reporting and realistic novel-writing. It is true that he writes: 'In answer to the question "Can you think of any literary work that is not in some sense a parable?" one has to recognise that nearly all "realistic" fiction must be so, in however slight a sense. . . . So the differences between "realistic writing" and "parable writing" appears to be one of degree. But,' he adds, 'the difference in degree can be so vast that as in many other spheres, it is convenient to use a rule of thumb and treat a really noticeable difference in degree as constituting a difference in kind.' No doubt; but there is a very great area of writing in which realism and parable can be said to overlap. One thinks, almost at random, of *Robinson Crusoe*, of *Great Expectations*, of the novels of Charlotte Bronte, even of *Madame Bovary*, or of a novel like *Esther Waters*, which is nothing if not a work of realism and even of naturalism and yet transcends what are normally regarded as the limits of naturalism because its heroine, for all the scrupulous fidelity with which she is depicted, carries with her in her effect upon what is now several generations of readers the aura of a figure of romance. That Moore himself was probably quite unaware of this is beside the point. Similarly, MacNeice who loved fairy stories, seems to have failed to see the fairy-story basis of many realistic novels. I am suggesting that in our time and for the past two hundred years it is through the novel that the romance has been transmitted. I conclude that MacNeice's view of the novel and of realism was inadequate, and in *Varieties of Parable* I suspect that in part he was blinded by his adaptation of the word 'parable'.

THE TRANSLATION OF
THE 'AGAMEMNON'
OF AESCHYLUS

W. B. STANFORD

MacNeice could hardly have chosen a more exacting exercise in classical interpretation than translating the *Agamemnon*. Its text is often uncertain or defective. Its language is opulent, highly metaphorical, and often tantalizingly obscure or ambiguous. (In modern times Gerard Manley Hopkins has, perhaps, come nearest to it.) Its style is profoundly symbolical with deep liturgical undertones. Its thought, though often conventional in substance, wrestles with the profoundest problems of human destiny. And its emotional climaxes are unsurpassed in any other Greek drama. Another serious difficulty is that Aeschylus frequently used the stiff archaic idioms of earlier Greek drama — the kind of thing that Housman parodied so scathingly in his *Fragment of a Greek Tragedy* beginning

> O suitably-attired-in-leather boots
> Head of a traveller, wherefore seeking whom
> Whence by what way how purposed art thou come
> To this well-nightingaled vicinity?

On the other hand, another attempt to translate the *Agamemnon* into English had the advantage that in 1936, when MacNeice completed his, there were no acknowledged masterpieces already in existence. Homer had his Chapman and Pope, Plutarch his North, and Euripides his Gilbert Murray. But Aeschylus still awaited a master-interpreter, despite many efforts by scholars and literary men — including Browning, Headlam and Gilbert Murray. (The grotesque contortions of Browning's version evoked enough ridicule to frighten off any but the boldest spirits outside the arena of scholarship. Tyrrell, the Dublin classical scholar, is said to have remarked that it was lucky the Greek was there to enucleate what Browning meant.)

MacNeice made it clear in his brief, uncompromising introduction that he was not aiming at literary distinction on the one hand or close word-for-word fidelity (like Eduard Fraenkel's later version) on the other:

> I have written this translation primarily for the stage. I have consciously sacrificed certain things in the original — notably the liturgical flavour of the diction and the metrical complexity of the choruses. It is my hope that the play emerges as a play and not as a museum piece.

He certainly succeeded in producing an eminently actable version. But much of the dramatic power of the *Agamemnon* comes from its poetic quality. Rendered in prosaic language the lyrical parts become tedious and the dramatic parts crude. If MacNeice had produced nothing more than an acting version, in the kind of plastic neutral-toned style that masterful producers like to handle— without having to worry about any literary flim-flam — then it would hardly have deserved more than a passing sigh for wasted time in any assessment of his work.

Let us look at a few examples. First, the Herald's description of how the Greek army suffered on its way to Troy and during its campaign there:

> If I were to tell of our labours, our hard lodging,
> The sleeping on crowded decks, the scanty blankets,
> Tossing and groaning, rations that never reached us —
> And the land too gave matter for more disgust,
> For our beds lay under the enemy's walls.
> Continuous drizzle from the sky, dews from the marshes,
> Rotting our clothes, filling our hair with lice.
> And if one were to tell of the bird-destroying winter
> Intolerable from the snows of Ida
> Or of the heat when the sea slackens at noon
> Waveless and dozing in a depressed calm. . . .

Second, a lyrical passage, the famous description of Iphigenia just before her sacrifice at Aulis:

> Then dropping on the ground her saffron dress,
> Glancing at each of her appointed
> Sacrificers a shaft of pity,
> Plain as in a picture she wished
> To speak to them by name, for often

At her father's table where men feasted
She had sung in celebration for her father
With a pure voice, affectionately, virginally,
The hymn for happiness at the third libation.

Third, one of the most puzzling and dark-textured passages in all
the dialogue of the play, Clytaemnestra's mysteriously symbolical
speech spoken while Agamemnon steps on to the crimson tapestries
that she has spread for him to tread as he goes to his doom inside
the accursed palace:

There is the sea and who shall drain it dry? It breeds
Its wealth in silver of plenty of purple gushing
And ever-renewed, the dyeings of our garments.
The house has its store of these by God's grace, King.
This house is ignorant of poverty
And I would have vowed a pavement of many garments
Had the palace oracle enjoined that vow
Thereby to contrive a ransom for his life.
For while there is root, foliage comes to the house
Spreading a tent of shade against the Dog Star.
So now that you have reached your hearth and home
You prove a miracle — advent of warmth in winter;
And further this — even in the time of heat
When God is fermenting wine from the bitter grape,
Even then it is cool in the house if only
Its master walk at home, a grown man, ripe.
O Zeus the Ripener, ripen these my prayers;
Your part it is to make the ripe fruit fall.

Fourth, a piece of philosophical lyric:

Truly when health grows much
It respects not limit; for disease,
Its neighbour in the next door room,
Presses upon it.
A man's life, crowding sail,
Strikes on the blind reef:
But if caution in advance
Jettison part of the cargo
With the derrick of due proportion,

> The whole house does not sink,
> Though crammed with a weight of woe
> The hull does not go under.
> The abundant bounty of God
> And his gifts from the year's furrows
> Drive the famine back.

These — readers will perhaps agree — are not merely competent verse, but genuinely poetic in a lean and sinewy way. In several places here and elsewhere MacNeice has simplified the meaning of the Greek for the sake of clarity, thereby losing a good deal in terms of thought-association and contrapuntal imagery (a favourite Aeschylean device). Occasionally, too, he lapses into translationese, as in

> O fortunes of this house
> Where not as before are things well
> ordered now.

In general tone he has fined down the texture of Aeschylus' diction to a smoother, more translucent surface. The result is like what has happened to the once highly coloured classical temples and statues. Time and weather have made their marble white, and we admire their shapes rather than their shape-and-colour. In fact MacNeice's version conforms better to our conventional idea of the classical style than Aeschylus' opulent and often exuberant Greek. Yet how much better this is than the Wardour Street, or Biblical, or Swinburnian, English of MacNeice's predecessors!

There are less tangible qualities, of course, that a good translation must convey. In the *Agamemnon* we must feel the growing sense of impending doom, the incandescent dynamism of Clytaemnestra, the doomed majesty of Agamemnon, the pathos of Cassandra who foresees all the agony, the helpless compassionate witness of the chorus, and much else. There is also the alternation of hope and fear, of light and darkness, and the preparation for the ultimate consummation of the whole trilogy. It would take a lengthy analysis to compare MacNeice adequately with Aeschylus in these qualities. Here the present writer can only say that he finds the total effect of MacNeice's version very satisfying and his fidelity to the general meaning of Aeschylus' Greek — though here there is bound to be scholastic disagreement on many points — consistently high.

THE 'FAUST' TRANSLATION:
A PERSONAL ACCOUNT

E. L. STAHL

In any assessment of Louis MacNeice's translation of Goethe's *Faust* it is necessary to know how it came to be made. Its merits are a measure of MacNeice's poetic skill: they are not directly associated with the occasion which prompted the inception of the work, while the imperfections are at least partly attributable to that occasion.

The work was conceived as a radio production to commemorate the two-hundredth anniversary of Goethe's birth in 1949. It was planned to consist of six programmes, each of about one hour's listening time.

There were some apparently insuperable initial difficulties. What Goethe conceived as a theatrical production had to be turned into a presentation in a related, but essentially different medium. Louis MacNeice belonged to the Features Department of the BBC: if he had been in the Drama Department, perhaps he would have given the translation a different character in certain important respects.

A technical difficulty of another kind was Louis MacNeice's deficient knowledge of the German language. Wystan Auden was first invited to undertake the task. When he declined, Louis took it on at short notice, provided I was employed as his 'textual consultant'. It was a daunting enterprise for both of us. We had only a few months to complete the work, but it did not take us long to find a *modus operandi* that suited us both. At Louis's London home or his office at the BBC and later in a sun-drenched, mistral-swept Provençal house lent to us by a friend, we went over the German text line by line, day by day after I had made rough oral or written prose versions. We then spent many hours discussing the meaning of individual words, phrases and passages, as well as the structure of the work as a whole. Thesaurus-like I plied Louis with synonyms and antonyms and with as many quotations and allusions as I could, however inadequately, muster, until he found what he con-

[67]

sidered the appropriate version or its near equivalent. Of course we had many differences of opinion. Some of them remained unresolved and Louis's choice of tone, phrase and rhythm had to prevail; some were set aside by, perhaps, not very satisfactory compromises. By and large, however, the co-operation was remarkably smooth; although we found it an exhausting experience, it was also a most rewarding one. I certainly gained deeper insights into Goethe's play than I had before and I sometimes wonder whether the arduous exercise Louis had to undergo in adopting and adapting Goethe's multifarious verse forms ('Knittelvers', blank verse, free verse, idiosyncratic two-beat lines, hexameters, trimeters, trochaic tetrameters, choric odes on the Greek model, alexandrines) had some effect upon his later practice.

What to begin with seemed to me the most disconcerting handicap, Louis's deficiency in German, eventually turned out to be no mean advantage. His powers of empathy in poetic matters were remarkable, but above all he could go his own way, freed, as he was, from the inhibitions of bilingual knowledge. He also liberated himself from the subtle dominance of other verse translations. At most he used a prose crib: he even forebore reading Shelley's superb fragment. By such means, I believe, he achieved, at some cost of accuracy, a translation which is also a piece of re-creation verging on creation itself by attaining a just balance between originality and reproduction.

Any production of Goethe's *Faust* for the stage is fraught with formidable tasks of cutting and compressing. This is true of Part 1 and of course in much greater measure for Part 2. The advantage a producer for the stage has over one for radio lies in the aid and effect he gains from the visual impressions. Apart from the words Louis MacNeice could rely only on sound-effects such as incidental music, tolling bells, ticking clocks, howling winds and rushing waters. He was obliged to work out as clear a structure of plot and character action as was consistent with retaining some of the chief characteristics of Goethe's masterpiece: the diversity of its dramatic, lyrical and narrative forms and the variations of mood, passionate, reflective, humorous by turn.

I believe Louis MacNeice solved this problem in the main with consummate skill. Many readers and listeners who knew Goethe's play in the original or from other translations criticised his abridgments which included Dedicatory Poem, the Prologue on the Stage, major portions of the two Walpurgis Night scenes and of

Acts I, III and IV in Part 2. A manifestly serious omission for the radio version was the exclusion of the incomparable Student scene (ll. 1868-2050) which was, however, restored for the printed version. The omission exemplifies one of the problems Louis MacNeice had to grapple with. He felt, no doubt rightly, that the introduction of a new voice at that stage of the dramatic action, just before Faust and Mephistopheles set out on their journey after the signing of the pact, might have confused listeners and generally detracted from the auditory effectiveness of the climax in the Study Room 2 scene.

A less important, but in its way characteristic excision is the passage on the armchair in Gretchen's room (ll. 2695 ff.). Louis felt this was not only distracting but unpleasantly mawkish. Here his critical predilections dictated the cut, just as they did in many passages in Act III of Part 2. While he had a soft spot for Mephistopheles, he censured Goethe for allowing Faust an excessive amount of 'bellyaching'. Most of all he took against Helena and was disparaging about her much as Stevie Smith was in *Novel on Yellow Paper*.

Another kind of impairment of Goethe's text, acquiesced in rather than approved of by me, is the interpolation of a bridging passage written by Louis himself. There seemed to him no other way in which the continuity of the action could be maintained, given the many cuts he had to make as well as the exigencies of his medium.

Inevitably much of the grand design of *Faust* got lost in Mac-Neice's translation. Goethe's gigantic work is not the formless conglomerate which, after the publication of the completed Part 2 in 1832, it was so long held to be. The structural entity of the entire drama has only fairly recently been fully perceived. Louis Mac-Neice was sensible of what he called the 'digressions and abandonments' of the drama, but he was less prepared to accept that it forms an entity composed of carefully planned devices such as repetition, symmetry, parallelism, contrast and a coherent pattern of symbols. Not the whole of Goethe's master-design is preserved in MacNeice's translation, yet at least he reproduced its unique combination of dramatic and lyrical effects.

There can be little doubt that the outstanding contribution he made is the rendering of the many and varied lyrical passages in both parts of *Faust*. He was not so successful in capturing the tone of the unsophisticated songs and ballads of Part 1, except when they are sardonic and irreverent. His unsurpassed achievements are his re-creations of the complex and subtle measures of such lyric masterpieces as the angelic choruses of both parts; Gretchen's elegiac prayer in the 'Zwinger' scene and her poignant visions in the dungeon; and the opening scene of Part 2.

Nowhere is that achievement more impressive than in the translation of the concluding lines of the whole work:

> Alles Vergängliche
> Ist nur ein Gleichnis;
> Das Unzulängliche,
> Hier wird's Ereignis;
> Das Unbeschreibliche,
> Hier ist's getan;
> Das Ewig-Weibliche
> Zieht uns hinan.

> All that is past of us
> Was but reflected;
> All that was lost in us
> Here is corrected;
> All indescribables
> Here we descry;
> Eternal Womanhead
> Leads us on high.

MacNeice took a very long time over this rendering of the *Chorus Mysticus*, elaborating and refining it during one of those extended phases of withdrawn and abstracted concentration when he conceived and shaped his best poetry. I experienced such fertile periods of his creativity over the years in unexpected places, as when he wrote a section of *Autumn Journal* in a Paris bar. He took especial pleasure in arriving at his bold rendering of Goethe's phrase 'das Ewig-Weibliche' having eschewed the current 'Eternal Feminine'. The neologism 'Womanhead' is a stroke of genius. Analogous to 'Godhead' this coinage admits the interpretation that man's ultimate transformation is consummated not by Womanhood at large but by its divine manifestation embodied in the Virgin. On a more terrestrial plane, at the end of Act II, Homunculus, Faust's diminutive mythic counterpart in transformation through striving, follows Galatea in order to 'evolve his higher forms and features'.

Louis MacNeice's ingenious solutions of very difficult problems of translation often led Wystan Auden to express his admiration and to voice regret that we did not cover the whole work. When at last Louis was freed from pressures of programme-making in the relaxed ambience of semi-retirement, he showed increasing willingness to undergo once more the rigours of translating *Faust*. Had he lived to do this, he might have come to appreciate the complete scope of Goethe's dramatic design, and produced a truly representative version of the whole work.

MACNEICE IN THE THEATRE

ALEC REID

In their bibliography of Louis MacNeice, Armitage and Clark note six plays for the theatre, three printed and three in manuscript. The translation of the *Agamemnon, Out of the Picture* and *One for the Grave* have all been published and professionally performed; *Station Bell* was put on by the Birmingham University Dramatic Society as an end of term play, *Blacklegs* was accepted by the Abbey Theatre, Dublin, but never staged, and *Eureka*, mentioned in the BBC archives but still unperformed. John Press in his study of MacNeice refers to *Traitors in Our Way*, presented by the Belfast Group Theatre, but, if the title is any guide, this may well be *Blacklegs* under another name.

Judged as isolated works of literature, none of the plays is outstanding and the detached critic, wise in his hindsight, may well be tempted to dismiss them as a comparatively minor part of MacNeice's achievement. But as MacNeice himself insisted, no poem can be validly considered without reference to its author and the world in which it was created. This principle holds for his own plays; while he was working on them they were as much a part of his life as his poetry or his criticism and unquestionably he put more of himself into them than into the commissioned pot-boilers of the later '30s, books undertaken, as he frankly admits, 'to show these commercial bastards that one knows the ropes as well as they do.' In February 1934 he had written to his friend, Anthony Blunt: 'This brings my total of books which I want published 1934-5 to 5: 1 Poems; 2 Novel; 3 Play; 4 Latin Humour; 5 Analytic Autobiography.' The play is not the first on the list, but neither is it the last.

At the time of this letter, MacNeice was passing through a crucial stage of development both as an individual and as an artist. For four and a half years he had been living in Birmingham, lecturing in Classics at the university, a job he had undertaken not from any sense of academic vocation but so that he could get married as soon as he had finished his finals at Oxford and, with his livelihood secured, could then pursue his real ambition — to become a writer. But the two-level strategy had not worked; from the outset the creative artist had been sacrificed almost entirely to the husband. With fatal ease, Louis and Mariette had locked themselves into a fantasy world of their own, totally absorbed the one with the other, not even spending a night apart in four years. Now he was coming gradually to realise that he could not write, as he put it, in a hot-house. 'I was aware of a dichotomy,' he wrote in *The Strings are False*, 'living with Mariette was not only pleasant but good . . . but outside Mariette was the Rest of the World, intellectually stimulating and in many ways more real than Mariette but horrifying.' In May, 1934, the first and only child of the marriage was born, and as MacNeice says, 'Instead of a prolonged elopement, I suddenly found I had a family.' But the dichotomy between his intellectual and domestic lives was to continue a little longer.

According to William T. McKinnon, the play MacNeice hoped to see published in 1934-5 is 'presumably' *Station Bell*. It had given him a great deal of trouble and was still unfinished by 8 June 1934. A note, probably in MacNeice's writing, attached to an imperfect copy of the play in the Library of the University of Texas at Austin reads 'completed c. 1935, performed by the Birmingham University Dramatic Society c. 1936.' Making all allowances for textual imperfections, *Station Bell* is a strange work. Written in an obviously 'Irish' idiom and set in Dublin in the near future, it centres on the seizure of political power by a female 'nationalist' dictator, Julia Brown, and on her unsatisfactory marriage to a tired but essentially humane and balanced academic. The other principal characters are a shabby military leader, a testy capitalist complete with saxophone, and a mad clergyman who is dispensing drink in a station bar in Act I and eloping for America with Julia in Act III. In between there is a very funny scene in which Julia and the General recruit a Propaganda Corps to represent the brave new Ireland. This includes a negro Celt who can dance an Irish jig, a mannequin complete with toy dog representing an ancient Irish wolf-hound, a conjurer, Séamus Stein, who materializes glasses of Guinness out of thin air, an epileptic drummer, and two Carnival giants.

The Birmingham production, with a cast including Walter Allen, R. D. Smith and Henry Reed, seems to have been a somewhat hasty affair. Writing in *The Mermaid*, the undergraduate magazine, for March 1937, the reviewer begins with Dr. Johnson's remark that the Irish are a fair people since they never speak well of each other. He goes on:

> Mr. MacNeice is fairness itself. And since his frankness is both flattering and amusing, we had an evening of high jinks with the Dublin dictatress, giants and generals. The play has slapstick, satire and moments of real tension. I could not tell how much the failure to knit together as a whole was due to the hasty charade-like production and how much to the author's liking for action on various planes and his tendency to do too many things at once. In retrospect it is possible to appreciate the device of reconciling the dictatress and her husband against the background of fumbling giants; in the theatre it can only be fidgety.

As we shall see, these comments would be echoed when MacNeice's next original play *Out of the Picture* was presented in London.

The note attached to the Texas manuscript describes *Station Bell* as 'an unpublished farce', and that is, perhaps, the best description of it. When he was working on it, however, MacNeice seems to have taken his play rather more seriously. 'I am afraid it wouldn't be allowed in the I.F.S. [Irish Free State],' he confides to Blunt, 'as De Val [de Valera] would take it personally.' Even more surprisingly he had hopes of a London production, mentioning 'A thing, I think, called the Group Theatre.' Some of the images and ideas in *Station Bell* appear later, the auctioning of a worthless society, the nightmare figure of a cripple swinging on his crutches, the fanlight over the hungry door, while the civilized if ineffectual Dr. Brown is probably a colleague, certainly a blood brother of the Professor who appears in *Blacklegs*. In the last analysis, however, *Station Bell* is a fantasy, written in a fantasy world that would soon end with ironic consistency. Late in 1935, without any warning, Mariette deserted MacNeice for an All-American footballer, shattering a seven-year idyll but removing at least one dichotomy.

With Mariette gone MacNeice turned to 'the Rest of the World', horrifying though it might be. For the first time in his life, perhaps, he let himself think more about large public issues — Fascism, unemployment, the threat of war — than about the details of his private existence. He revived old friendships, cemented new ones, began to get about — in short, returned to that everyday world which was essential to him as a writer. There was nothing now to keep him in Birmingham, so he resigned his lectureship at the university and, without undue difficulty, found himself a similar job in London, starting with the new academic year. He also became directly involved with the Group Theatre, not through *Station Bell* but something very different — a translation in modern verse of the *Agamemnon* of Aeschylus, undertaken especially for them. McKinnon seems to suggest that MacNeice had started it in 1935. On 24 May 1936, soon after his first visit to Spain, he wrote to Blunt: 'Dodds [i.e. his friend Professor E. R. Dodds] wants me to revise Agamemnon some more, and then he says it will be rather remarkable.' He reports that T. S. Eliot, a director of Faber & Faber, is also interested in it. In the same letter MacNeice adds that he and Auden will drive to Stratford next day to meet Rupert Doone and Robert Medley, respectively producer and designer for the Group Theatre.

The Group Theatre had come into being as far back as 1932, when several young professional actors and actresses had banded themselves into an experimental company aiming at a new kind of play, a new style of production and a new management policy. In November 1933 the minutes of the Group Theatre contain a statement of its aesthetic:

> Its aim can be expressed in three words: A UNIFIED THEATRE. That is to say, a theatre which shall not be controlled by an IMPRESSARIO interested primarily in PROFIT: A STAR ACTOR interested primarily in his or her own prestige: A PRODUCER interested primarily in NOVEL EFFECTS: a DESIGNER interested primarily in SPECTACLE, but by a CO-OPERATIVE EFFORT which shall put the THEATRE as a whole above any of its parts.

In pursuit of these objects, the directors, including Auden, determined to draw every element of a production — the text, the music, the décor, the dancing — from within the Group. As a start, Doone, himself the last male dancer to have been trained by Diagheliev, invited Auden to write a ballet and a play on the same theme — Orpheus in the Underworld. As he worked on them, the two projects fused to form a political masque — *The Dance of Death*. This had been staged in 1934 on two successive Sundays in the Everyman Theatre, Hampstead, had been quickly followed by Eliot's *Sweeney Agonistes* and by Auden and Isherwood's *The*

Dog Beneath the Skin, also written specially for the Group. In 1935, the company felt strong enough to mount a season of repertory in the West End at the Westminster Theatre. Here, it is pleasant to imagine MacNeice, up from Birmingham for the Irish International Rugby match at Twickenham, may have seen their work for the first time. The interests of the Group were by no means confined to poetic or literary drama. It had set up a practical film section directed by Basil Wright, had staged lectures, seminars and dance recitals, after one of which Hedli Anderson (who was to marry MacNeice in 1942) sang some of her latest cabaret songs. There was a Summer School, in the manner of the Fabian Society. A *Group Theatre Paper*, started in June 1936, kept its members posted with details of exhibitions, and with news of other socially committed theatres like the Unity. Art in any form was seen as a social responsibility. W.H.A., for instance, wrote in a piece called 'Selling the Group Theatre' — 'An experimental theatre ought to be regarded as normal and useful a feature of normal life as an experimental laboratory.'

The idea for the *Agamemnon* may have come from Auden or just as possibly from Doone himself, since he had a great admiration for the play. 'I do not respect it,' he was later to proclaim, 'I love it.' In the first *Group Theatre Paper* published in June the *Agamemnon* is announced as the opening event of the autumn programme and in July MacNeice is seeking Blunt's advice about a good artist to design the drop-curtain for it. In the event, the *Agamemnon* was not produced until November but in the meanwhile the *Group Theatre Papers* are full of it. There are numerous extracts, Doone explains the ideas underlying his production, and there is a lengthy discussion of the masks, designed by Medley. In the September *Theatre Paper*, A.W. writes:

> The Greek vase is so dusty with centuries of official approbation that we forget that it still contains powerful wine. The Group Theatre believes that Louis MacNeice's translation of Aeschylus' *Agamemnon* and Rupert Donne's production of it will be as interesting to a London audience of 1936 as it was stimulating to the Athenians of 458 B.C.
>
> MacNeice is a young poet who is very much of this age. That he should be so stirred by the poetic drama of Aeschylus as to undertake the formidable and fascinating task of retranslating it into his own idiom is a significant fact. In reading

his version you are so constantly struck by the contemporary turn of thought and imagery that you might suspect MacNeice was merely writing modern variations on a theme by Aeschylus. But turn back to the original, and you will find that he has followed the Greek with the utmost faithfulness.

The *Agamemnon* was presented at the Westminster Theatre on Sunday, 1 November, and Sunday, 8 November, 1936. Donne dressed his chorus of Argive elders in dinner jackets — 'the uniform of the audience' — as he explained in a programme note — and gave them masks reminiscent of the coloured glass of church windows relative to the religion of Aeschylus' play. The main characters did not wear masks, but the monkish atmosphere of the play was carried through in the choreography, the Minotaur, the Bull, the Owl, the Bat, the Gorgon's Head, the Harpies, danced round like devils while Aegisthus and Clytemnestra walked in the moonlight. The music was by Benjamin Britten, and MacNeice himself was heard quoting from the Greek.

As might have been expected, it provoked sharply contrasting reaction. W. B. Yeats remarked to Professor Dodds that they were assisting at the death of tragedy, though this applied, seemingly, to the production rather than the text which Yeats is said to have admired. W. A. Darlington writing in the *Daily Telegraph* jocularly headed his piece *Group Theatre Orgy* subtitled it 'Aeschylus, thou art translated', and ended by confessing that he had not seen 'such a funny piece of footle for months'. *The Observer* critic H.H. found it 'impossible to be bored by the play though difficult to be consistently impressed.' *The Times* felt the production worth a thoughtful and authoritative notice running to close on a column, finally ranking it as 'another distinguished failure to recreate in English the masterpiece of ancient tragedy'.

MacNeice was now living in London. He had left Birmingham in July, spent August with Auden in Iceland, and had returned to a flat in Keats Grove, Hampstead. Here, as he says in *The Strings are False*, 'began a life which was a whirl of narcotic engagements — meetings for a drink, political meetings, private views, flirtations, experimental theatre, the question of my overdraft, the question of Spain.' His association with the Group did not end with the *Agamemnon*. Two weeks after its second performance, he and Rupert Doone read in the Society's clubrooms a dialogue which he had written on the necessity for an active tradition and experiment in the theatre. 'The problem we are up against,' he began, 'is the problem of identity and difference. It is essential for human beings to change and develop, but it is essential that they shall remain the same human beings, otherwise they would not appreciate their own development.' He goes on to speak of W. B. Yeats who, he argued, had tried to save the poetic drama but had failed. Yeats was too reactionary: the values in his plays belonged to a world which had passed away and his dialogue, though admirably clear and simple, was not modern verse. On the other hand, Yeats, like Auden and Eliot, was right to suggest that the study of individual character does not belong to tragedy but to the novel. The Dialogue ends with a parable, not a very impressive example but a pointer to one very significant future development. The last Group paper of 1936 mentions two forthcoming events — Auden and Isherwood's *The Ascent of F6* and 'a new play by Louis MacNeice'. The next issue prints the final chorus of this, thereby identifying it as *Out of the Picture*.

MacNeice had put a good deal of work into this play before he left Birmingham. In the letter of 24 May 1936, announcing his trip to Stratford with Auden, he had written to Blunt: 'My play about Venus is near done — a draft I mean' and a few weeks later, perhaps as a result of his meeting with Doone and Medley, he was able to report that *The Rising Venus*, as it was now called, was to come out in the Spring. Faber and Faber, who had already accepted the *Agamemnon*, published it in June, 1937, under the title *Out of the Picture*; a note between the dedication page and the list of characters states that the play 'is to be performed during the summer of 1937 by the Group Theatre and Rupert Doone, with music by Benjamin Britten and sets and costumes by Robert Medley'. As with *The Dog Beneath the Skin*, published by Faber two years earlier, this promise was to prove a pious hope; in fact *Out of the Picture* did not open until 2 December 1937, again for two performances and again at the Westminster Theatre.

As with *Station Bell*, MacNeice is here an original playwright as distinct from a translator, responsible for plot, characterisation, and language. In some ways, *Out of the Picture* shows an advance on the earlier play. MacNeice no longer feels the need of introductory descriptions such as 'the Girl, nasty little type, the sort that evokes the sadist.' to establish his characters; he has forsaken the broad, localised, Irish turn of phrase for the elliptical, staccato wit of the new poets. The plot, however, still seems to work on two levels, and, as *Station Bell* is coloured by the fantasy world of the Birmingham idyll, so *Out of the Picture* reflects the dramatic themes and political preoccupation of Auden, the Group Theatre and the intellectual Left of the 'thirties. Coming after *The Dance of Death, The Dog Beneath the Skin* and *The Ascent of F6, Out of the Picture* seems to conform to a familiar pattern. The review of it in *Scrutiny*, therefore, is no surprise.

> Mr. MacNeice has written a verse play. The verse might as well have been dispensed with. *Out of the Picture* is possibly good theatre — bad plays are sometimes good theatre — since it has a certain Hollywood slickness and all the paraphernalia of an Auden play, radio announcers, choruses, parodies of hymnal tunes, and cardboard comic types. Indeed but for the example of Auden one feels the play would not have been written. Unfortunately, the wit of the dialogue rarely matches Auden at his lowest level and the general *danse macabre* is quite unrealised. Even as the comic fails to be witty, the criticism fails to be serious.

On the surface, the indictment is true in each particular, yet if we concentrate too much on the apparent Auden, we may well miss the essential MacNeice. Just as in politics, philosophy and psychology, he had always stood a little apart from his contemporaries, had never quite been a part of the new school, so now in his verse-play he does something rather different. According to Doone, in the mid-'thirties, the Group was aiming not at portraiture but at cartoons. MacNeice takes the conventional, almost obligatory swipes at the stock figures — the arrogant psychologist, the cynical materialist, the irresponsible politician — but *Out of the Picture* is the story of two individuals, James Portwright, an incompetent painter, and Moll O'Hara, his highly practical model. They are, unmistakably, individuals — portraits as Donne would say: their concerns are strictly immediate and personal — getting back a picture seized by the bailiffs, falling in love — things quite beyond any cartoon. A 1937 audience can easily be forgiven for thinking that *Out of the Picture* is about the coming Armageddon and the end of civilized society; we would do well, however, to remember that from the beginning MacNeice saw it as his 'Venus play' and in it he has a great deal to say about the nature of love. The title of the play is a kind of verbal conjuring trick; 'the picture' in it has nothing to do with the Portwright Venus but with the insignificance of the individual in a world fast drifting to destruction. Perhaps, in a way, MacNeice had been overtaken by the march of events. The play, probably begun in Birmingham in 1935, is about the feelings of an artist for two women and their response to him; in the London of 1937, however, the threat of imminent doom was obviously uppermost in the audiences' thoughts.

The critic of *The Times* was quick to point out that *Out of the Picture* was seeking to work on two levels, just as the reviewer in *The Mermaid* had said of *Station Bell*. '. . . its weakness lies not in dealing in abstraction but in trying to crowd in far more concrete and personal patterns than even so loose a form can hold and remain a form.' He also remarked that the diffusion of interest over a wide stage brings out a number of clear-cut and amusing sketches rather than any sustained and progressive performances. This point was emphasised in *The Daily Telegraph*: 'Mr. Louis MacNeice is not a dramatist, and as a pageant-writer he suffers from rhetorical excess. His effects are too long on their way, and the inconsequential bits only rarely justify their inclusion.' *The Sunday Times* critic found himself in two minds. The story of Portwright and Moll he sees as only a thread to give some kind of cohesion to a more general warning; 'not only the artist but all who belong to a regulated, agreeable life are nowadays "out of the picture" '. He goes on:

> This disagreeable truth is driven home in the manner successfully employed by Mr. Auden and Mr. Isherwood: burlesque, satire, music-hall turns, poetry within the same frame, comedy breaking into melodrama, revue, put to serious uses. In Act I the method is so successful that one begins to think it may become an established contribution to the theatre. Act II goes to bits; no hack writer of melodrama could do worse than Mr. MacNeice when his characters become human and shoot.

These are hard words, but, like several other critics, the writer found it impossible to be angry with *Out of the Picture*. Even at the worst, it had moments of poetry, truth, and wit; it was produced cleverly and sometimes brilliantly by Rupert Doone; all in all, the impression is not of a distinguished failure as with the *Agamemnon*, but of an agreeable flop.

For one critic, however, it was much more. For H.H. in *The Observer*, MacNeice was a poet, coming to the theatre less to divert than to chasten.

> Though he affects to tether his scenes to earth by laying them in studios, surgeries, sale-rooms, and flats, they give glimpses both of heaven and hell; . . . His backchat, his incidental burlesque, mask a divine discontent with the blindness, the greed, the casual folly of men who, through war, would encompass their own destruction. . . . One feels at times that this poet, sceptical perhaps of his instrument, uses the theatre awkwardly. The mixture of sacred and profane is not too smooth, and some of its more playful elements jar. But the play contains enough true poetry and righteous indignation to absolve its crudities and make the performance memorable.

Once again MacNeice seemed to find himself confronted with a dichotomy. On the one hand, by virtue of his work at the Group and, according to Walter Allen, by virtue of his essay, *Modern Poetry*, MacNeice had firmly aligned himself with the committed poets of the Left, Auden, Spender and Day Lewis. On the other, to quote MacNeice himself in *The Strings are False*, written some four years afterwards, 'I continued dreaming about bombs and the fascists, was worried over women, was mortifying my aesthetic sense by trying to write as Wystan [Auden] did, without bothering too much with finesse (witness *Out of the Picture*), was bothering not to bother.' From this confusion emerged two major achievements, the essay *Modern Poetry* and *Autumn Journal*, as well as the spate of trivial commissioned work, and possibly one play (the unpublished and unperformed) *Blacklegs*.

At first sight this might well have been written in Birmingham for it has about it the same kind of fantasy as in *Station Bell*. The action is set in the near future, during a war involving Hitler and a General Strike. The scene is set, not in a railway station refreshment room, but on a builder's scaffold half-way up a steeple. The characters speak the same kind of broad 'Irish' dialect, and one of them is a Professor who could well be Dr. Brown himself. Only two things suggest that *Blacklegs* might have come later. In the first *Group Theatre Paper* of 1936 G. B. describing the Unity Theatre production of *Waiting for Lefty* by Clifford Odets, writes, 'Odets might seem among the first to evolve a new drama directly from the ritual of the political platform, as, in the Middle Ages, our present drama was directly evolved from the ritual of the Church', a description perfectly fitting *Blacklegs* with its discussion of the motives behind strike-breaking, and its conflict between private values and class solidarity. Secondly, according to Armitage and Clark, the manuscript of the play at Austin in Texas, suggests that it was accepted by the Abbey Theatre in Dublin in 1939 but was never performed.

But *Blacklegs* and its date are matters of small account as, one suspects, is *Eureka*, still unpublished though considered by the BBC shortly after the war. Far more important, in 1938, MacNeice, in *Modern Poetry*, conceded that 'Poets' plays have so far hardly been successful as plays.' As J. C. Trewin citing Norman Marshall has said, none of the Group's authors showed any real sense of the theatre or an ability to write dramatic poetry; MacNeice himself admits that 'some form [of verse] is required half way between the healthy but vulgar hodge-podge of Auden and Isherwood and the arid dignity of Spender.' A few lines later he writes: 'Poets, however, should be encouraged to write dramatic verse as they should be encouraged to write narrative verse or occasional verse.' Then, with fascinating prescience, he goes on: 'It is particularly likely that they may find a good medium in radio plays.'

He could not have spoken more truly. Twenty years were to pass before MacNeice next attempted a play for the theatre, and in that time he had written about one hundred pieces for broadcasting, mastering and helping to shape a whole new art form. But the world of 1958 and *One for the Grave* was radically different from that of 1937 and *Out of the Picture*. Hitler and Mussolini were dead, Hiroshima had dwarfed Guernica, the Welfare State had anticipated the Marx Utopia. Poetry was now on the defensive; Auden, Spender and Day Lewis, though still alive, were fast sinking into Establishment figures. By contrast, MacNeice was widely regarded, in the words of one critic, as 'played out', having reached his peak with *Autumn Journal*, published in March 1939. Had he not frankly admitted that, as a poet he had reached a 'middle stretch'? Why should he now revert to a stage play with all the gimmicks, the revue sketches, the parodies, the backchat, the general slickness of *Out of the Picture*?

The answer is to be found in the first of the Clark Lectures given by MacNeice at Cambridge in 1963, and published posthumously as *Varieties of Parable*, a book standing in the same relation to the end of his creative life as *Modern Poetry* had to the early part. MacNeice argues that the essence of parable is the creation of a special 'inner world' — an occupation which he, as an inveterate dreamer, a lyrical poet, and a practitioner of sound radio, finds peculiarly attractive. But, unlike the cartoon world of the satirist or the propagandist, the 'inner world' of the parabolist must correspond to that external world which we all know. The television studio in *One for the Grave* is immediately recognisable as such but it is also the world we live in. The programme we are watching, like every other programme, is controlled by a Floor Manager who cues his actors on and off, and whose authority on floor-level is absolute. Here, however, the floor is also Earth, the floor manager's name is Morty, and he is Death. This is the direct antithesis of the railway buffet with its clerical barman in *Station Bell*, or the vaulted marmoreal auction-rooms in *Out of the Picture*, where the bids can rise from three guineas and a course of psychoanalysis through three guineas and a black cat to three guineas and an actress's autograph.

Only through parable, or double-level writing, MacNeice feels, can the poet or dramatist cope with the 'inner conflicts'—of identity, for instance, or of purpose — which are becoming more and more recognised in the world of today. At present, he admits, parable writing is still something practised only by a minority, but a growing and important one. 'There is something in the world today that makes me turn back to Spenser and Spenser, for me, can throw light on Beckett and on Golding. [Two of the major modern parabolists he has already cited.] Perhaps the converse is also true.' As a stage dramatist, MacNeice had first come to general notice with an attempt to re-create a classical tragedy for a twentieth-century audience, an attempt which *The Times* called 'a distinguished failure'. His last stage work was equally experimental for it tried to turn a mediaeval form, the Morality Play, into meaningful contemporary theatre. It, likewise, was not wholly successful, but we must remember that MacNeice had left it unrevised; had he lived he would certainly have shortened and refined it. He had once complained that Eliot's *Murder in the Cathedral* is not properly a play since its ending is known from the beginning. The same objection could be raised to *One for the Grave* but this play does not depend on suspense for its effect: it impresses by a certain sombre dignity transcending all its blemishes — even as Everyman himself does.

Its importance may well lie in what it tells us about MacNeice himself. Many of the incidents are autobiographical and frequently the voice of Everyman is unmistakably the voice of MacNeice. Perhaps he allowed more of himself to come through here than in the more carefully-worked poems. The lasting impression is of a sustained stoicism. Everyman has indulged his weaknesses, has often fallen pitifully short, has lost in a rigged game, yet at the end he goes, leaving us strangely comforted. *One for the Grave* in a way sums up MacNeice's achievement as a playwright. It leaves us thinking of him as an experimental dramatist, responding to developments around him, not particularly successful, but not to be written off. In Everyman's last words, 'I thank Thee for giving me the chance. . . . If I failed to use it, forgive me.'

The quotations from MacNeice's letters appear in *Apollo's Blended Dream* by William T. McKinnon, Oxford University Press, to whom the present author gladly acknowledges his debt.

CASTLE ON THE AIR

R. D. SMITH

The wavelengths that I use are the wavelengths of the heart
And anyone — who has the right heart — can hear me.
(Radio Script: 'Salute to the New Year')

MacNeice was thirty-three when he joined the BBC's crack department, Features, on 26 May 1941, and not quite fifty-six when he
died on 3 September 1963. So (with short leaves of absence and
reporting trips that took him to India, Pakistan, Ceylon, the U.S.A.,
N. Ireland, S. Africa, Greece, France and Ghana) his trade for over
twenty years was that of radio writer-producer. A brief venture
into TV, like his hopes for theatrical success, did not come off.

> To work. To my own office, my own job,
> Not matching pictures, but inventing sound,
> Precalculating microphone and knob

> In homage to the human voice. To found
> A castle on the air requires a mint
> Of golden intonations and a mound

> Of typescript in the trays.
> (*Autumn Sequel*)

There is a great deal of typescript; I've handled over 150 scripts
in the BBC Play Library, and I believe there may be others that got
away. Many are thirty minutes long, but many more much longer,
and after the start of the Third Programme in 1946 they generally
run over the hour. There were also translations mainly from the
Greek, and of Goethe's *Faust*.

Many of the scripts are of interest mainly to the historian. The
themes and occasions prompting them were topical and many of

the programmes were designed as propaganda. An anthology of extracts illustrated with photographs from *Picture Post* would vividly recreate daily life in the war years.

Not that MacNeice looked for a post in propaganda. 'There must be plenty of people to propagand, so I have no feeling of guilt in refusing to mortify my mind,' he wrote to Professor E. R. Dodds on 24 September 1939. A trip to the U.S.A. soon after, though both his loving and his lecturing were successful there, did not insulate him from the moral problems raised at home by the 'phoney war'. In a crucial letter to Mrs. Dodds, on 22 March 1940, he said: 'freedom means Getting Into Things, not getting Out of Them; also that one must keep making things which are *not oneself*, e.g. works of art.' He decided he must come home and help fight the war because, as he wrote to me 'I thought I was missing history.' He enquired about service in the Royal Navy, partly because he had no taste for military routine and would have had no physical aptitude for the R.A.F., and probably because his great friend Graham Shepard was a Lieutenant R.N.V.R., on North Atlantic convoy duty. He was told his eyesight was no good, a fact he and Auden had recorded about themselves in *Letters from Iceland*, 'Our four eyes that cannot see for nuts.' So he settled for the risk of mortifying his mind, and plunged into the BBC, to work on the Beat-the-Nazis campaign.

His first script was written some ten weeks before he signed on with the BBC. I guess that the interval was spent by E. A. Harding (the Harrap of *Autumn Sequel*) and Laurence Gilliam, Head of Features (the Herriot) in going through the administration hoops to obtain government permission to give civilian employment to a man of military age.

THE WAR YEARS (1941-1945)

Every trick and turn of radio-*drama* technique had already been discovered and exploited before the end of the 'twenties, by Richard Hughes, Lance Sieveking, and Tyrone Guthrie. Their devices of internal monologue, the swift, sharp-cut cinema reel of a life flashing through the mind of a dying person, sound effects verbally placed and primed, music as function not decoration, had been available to the poet for most of his writing life, as a glance at his play *Out of the Picture* shows: but radio-documentary had for inspiration only D. G. Bridson's epic in verse, ballads, and music

The March of the '45, a model as specialised as it is admirable. So in 1941 there was still much to be learned here, and it was in writing wartime documentaries that MacNeice learnt his craft.

It was common for would-be writers for radio to think that any old essay, monologue, or lecture could be made broadcast-worthy by writing in the margin against paragraph one, Narrator I, against paragraph two, Narrator II, and against paragraph three, Narrator III: if they were imaginative and bold they might add to one of these instructions — (female). But radio, like other, more stringently demanding arts, can only operate within decently observed conventions. One of these (and perhaps the most important in radio documentary) is that each voice speaking to the listener (one listener at a time) must have a character, a function, and its own individual rhythm, tone and accent. MacNeice, like most, though not all poets, realised this from the start. His sense of shape, his search for harmony, no less than his diligent copiousness, and verbal and rhythmic facility were to bring excitement and inspiration to a rather dull writing scene.

A fine example of MacNeice's documentary style was No. 26 in the series *The Stones Cry Out*. The earlier programmes had been set in London but now the scene moves to Northern Ireland, to Belfast. *A Home in Belfast* starts with strings and a singer giving out 'The Blue Hills of Antrim'. After recreating the hardworking life of Belfast, the obstinate love its people have for it, even amidst the bombed ruins of their homes and workplaces, MacNeice writes a bitter (and to-day even more poignant) parody of the song.

> The blue hills of Antrim look lazily down,
> On factory and foundry, on harbour and town,
> The hammers they fall and the shuttles they fly
> And the smoke of the chimneys goes up to the sky.
>
> The bad days are come for ourselves and our sons,
> The high hills of Antrim are noisy with guns,
> The men in the yards and the girls at the loom
> Are working in darkness and walking with doom.
>
> But still there's a prospect for you and for me
> Where the blue hills of Antrim look over the sea
> That the shadow will pass and the terror be gone
> And the life of Belfast will go peacefully on. . . .

MRS. GREEN   Ya's best stay here Eddie; ya know you've no-where to go. There's a bed ye can have to yourself, it'll be no trouble at all —

MR. GREEN   Ya can save your breath Sarah. The lad's asleep.

MRS. GREEN   Would ya believe that! It's a good thing too. He's awful upset with his sister and all and the ould house down to the ground —

MR. GREEN   He'll get over it in time.

MRS. GREEN   I'll get the bed fixed for him now. Aye, he'll get over it. He's young. Now, where did I put that pillow? Aye, he's young.

MR. GREEN   It's hard on the young too.

MRS. GREEN   Sure it's hard on all of us. But I think he'll feel better in the morning.

SINGER   The streets are in Darkness, the Lagan is Dark,
The guns on the concrete are ready to bark,
But the high hills of Antrim stand by to enfold
The poor and the broken, the young and the old.

Down there in the city they dream in the night
Of a wonderful future, a vision of light,
And the hills up above with a murmur of
      streams —
The blue hills of Antrim approve of their dreams.

A moving end; the script would stand broadcasting to-day without a comma changed.

In later radio *dramas* the poet explored his taste for romance and fantasy. After *The Dark Tower* probably his best known radio work is *Christopher Columbus*. It was produced in October, 1942, by Dallas Bower, since it was considered too grand a production job for the still inexperienced MacNeice to handle, probably because of the complications of dealing with the specially composed music by William Walton, which involved the use of the BBC Chorus and three soloists and guitarist.

The programme was set up to celebrate the 450th anniversary of the discovery of America. MacNeice used a spare epic treatment, with simplified and stylised characters, and choric interludes: 'I used for the dialogue an irregular blank verse based upon the rhythms of ordinary speech but capable of being heightened or tightened, flattened or bepurpled to requirements. The lyrics on the other hand I wrote in a regular form and made very simple in sentence structure and imagery because they were designed to be sung.'

The next major achievement was *He Had a Date*, an elegy for his friend Lt. Graham Shepard, R.N.V.R., killed on convoy duty in the North Atlantic. MacNeice's grief compelled a disciplined tightness in the writing; the complexity of the memories of the adolescent life they had shared drew from him terrifying images that prowled through his nightmares.

The tin-fish torpedo strikes: the anti-hero goes down, down; his past flashes across the last seconds of consciousness: and his nursery terror, the jack-in-the-box, pops up as death sweeps over the drowning man. The hero had felt himself a failure; now he had redeemed himself by keeping his date. His life had been a succession of near-misses. The tin-fish had not missed, and he did not miss being there to meet it.

MacNeice was to develop and objectify this theme in his masterpiece, *The Dark Tower*, which he wrote as the war ended: it was pre-recorded soon after V.J. Day, and transmitted in early 1946: the free world had endured: it had managed to 'hold that note at the end'.

THE POST-WAR YEARS (1946-50)

The Dark Tower extends and raises the realism of *He Had a Date* into a generalised universal world of parable, in which the logic of dream exists side by side with the logic of life. Once again a hero who cannot wholly commit himself to the role his family and his society have cast him for, yet resists all temptations, including the final one of doubt, and keeps his date with his destiny. Like Browning's Roland he comes to The Dark Tower to face the

Dragon, the ultimate evil, and, perhaps, to meet his own death. His is a Pilgrim's Progress, and a Quest.

Other later Morality Quest plays follow a kind of contemporary Everyman through the snares and temptations that modern civilization sets for intellectual and professional people: they often strain the listener's credulity by imposing too heavy a load of allegory or parable on structures of topical reference not strong enough to bear them. In *The Dark Tower* all the strains and tensions between its different levels are in equipoise.

In his introduction to *The Dark Tower*, MacNeice refuted the criticism that the parable play had become outdated after *Everyman*, *The Faerie Queene* and *Pilgrim's Progress* by reference to *Peer Gynt*, Kafka and *The Magic Mountain*, 'where though the disguise of "realism" is maintained, and nothing happens that is quite inconceivable in life, it is still the symbolic core which makes the work important'. This belief is central to all his work.

> My own impression is that pure "realism" is in our time almost played out, though most works of fiction of course will remain realistic *on the surface*. The single-track mind and the single-plane novel or play are almost bound to falsify the world in which we live. The fact that there is method in madness and the fact that there is fact in fantasy (and equally fantasy in 'fact') have been brought home to us not only by Freud and other psychologists but by events themselves. This being so, reportage can no longer masquerade as art.
>   . . . The dual-plane work will not normally be allegory in the algebraic sense; i.e. it will not be desirable or even possible to equate each of the outward and visible signs with a precise or rational inner meaning.

A great many of the themes in *The Dark Tower* are central to MacNeice's experience: many of the stage properties are life-long familiars, and they illustrate some of his deepest preoccupations. His anti-hero, Roland, sees through the family tradition, he sees through his mother's domination, he sees the dangers and disadvantages of the course he is destined to take, but he goes on with it. He goes to meet his end, tin-fish, dragon, or whatever that end may be.

I have heard MacNeice say more than once in bars when some smart alec had been confidently debunking something or other, 'If you always see through things you never see into them.' He was expressing the analytic, critical, sceptical part of himself, and, in the same phrase was declaring a belief in the need to make sense of the phenomena of life. His poems show how he delighted in the variety and flow and surface and shape and colour of things, and how, at the same time, he tried to look through the surface *dazzle* into them, and to see how the flux related to the permanance.

One of the themes that is central to him is an awareness, as he or Auden says in *Letters From Iceland*, of the 'gulf between Ideal and Real'.

> And to the good, who know how wide the gulf, how deep
> Between Ideal and Real, who being good have felt
> The final temptation to withdraw, sit down and weep,
> We pray the power to take upon themselves the guilt
> Of human action, though still as ready to confess
> The imperfection of what can and must be built,
> The wish and power to act, forgive, and bless.

The last part of this is, I think, Auden on his knees in rhetorical prayer, but the first part, I believe, is a close statement by Mac-Neice. His poetry was the means by which he made sense of, and put some meaning and order into his life, some harmony and pattern. And this he felt was tied up with belief. He says in the introduction to *The Dark Tower*: 'I have my beliefs and they permeate *The Dark Tower*, but do not ask me what "ism" it illustrates or what solution it offers. You don't normally ask for such things in the single plane work, why should they be forced upon something much more complex? Look, you know how unworthy a thing you make of me. What is life useful for anyway?'

In 1949 MacNeice was largely absorbed by the mammoth task of translating 8,000 lines of Goethe's *Faust*, adapting them for radio, and then working on the production. There was also a monumental creation in which he wrestled with many of the devils that tempted him in nightmares, and struggled to create a dramatic objective-correlate to his emotional, intellectual and social burrowings. This was *The Queen of Air and Darkness*, the fatal fated queen of A. E. Housman's poem, which MacNeice linked with the crisis in Tennyson's 'The Lady of Shalott', when 'The mirror crack'd from side to side;/"The curse has come upon me," cried/ The Lady of Shalott.'

Blind, with two handmaids to report to her what they can see happening in a mirror on the world outside, the Queen, who points the bone, or puts her finger on one man in each generation, and 'has him in thrall' for evil, listens avidly for news of the progress of her victim-protégés. They, evil incarnate, succeed each other as dictators; each at first a creative, sensitive, caring man, proceeds to butchery and beastliness. Her last victim, after his inevitable fall, descends to the Hall of the Catacombs, where the 'political prisoners' — all decent men and women who had opposed his tyranny — had been sent to rot. In adversity he discovers the agent of his degradation, and fighting his way to her mirror, which is at the end of the Catacombs, apocalyptically he cracks it open. The blind devil-goddess, believing to the last in her power, is vanquished: the anti-hero, from the depths of Hell has saved his soul, and the freedom of humanity.

THE LAST YEARS

At the end of his life MacNeice turned again to the morality. In the last year and a half of his life he was writing those strange, grave-haunted poems that appeared as *The Burning Perch*. He said he hadn't been aware of how much so many of them were obsessed with death. At the same time he did much studio work, reviving *Faust*, doing programmes on *Quasimodo*, *Latin Poetry* and on *Medieval Latin Poetry*. 'In my end is my beginning', though not quite. Just before his fatal illness three weeks later, came his last fine play *Persons from Porlock*.

It was a carbon copy, in subject and treatment of the earlier moralities. It lacks the heartbreaking immediacy of the first of all, *He Had a Date*, but it achieved what he had consistently worked for, and had till now, only intermittently managed; a tautness of structure, an economy of scene setting, a totally controlled story-line, and a *dramatic* realisation of character that had eluded him in those of the earlier scripts which had tried to synthesise contemporary man with the hero, or anti-hero of fable, folk and fairy-tale.

In such formalised plays as *Columbus* and *The Dark Tower*, nuances and contradictions in characters would have been inappropriate.

He had to go deep down to find what he needed, deep into the pot-holes and the caves: he went through the surface into hell, and found — we do not know what he found. He died on 3 September

1963, of a chill caught on the job while accompanying the recording engineers underground.

> By Loch Failure and Loch Sorrow and Loch Evil we must go
> Where the storm clouds are brooding on the wave
> For whatever else we know not there is one sure thing we
>   know:
> We must all take the high road to the Grave.

MacNeice was a splendid colleague: he never failed to do his corner, and he never missed a deadline: he had a date: he did not miss it.

MACNEICE:
SOUND AND VISION

DALLAS BOWER

There are critics of Louis MacNeice's work who say he sacrificed his integrity as poet when he 'sold out to the BBC'. Such an assertion is, of course, scarcely worth serious enquiry. By this yardstick, Wagner can be said to have 'sold out' to Ludwig II of Bavaria when he accepted that King's patronage in order to mount *Tristan und Isolde* in Munich and complete the composition of *Der Ring des Nibelungen* for Bayreuth. Many of MacNeice's radio scripts show a high quality of good verse and in those many instances when fine poetry emerges from them, the poet himself would confound any critic who contended he had not achieved the Aeschylean level wrongly expected of him, by suggesting the critic had misunderstood the premise from which the work had sprung.

The radio play as a genuine form had emerged rapidly as indeed had the silent cinema; it lacked a visual counterpart as the latter lacked an aural. Very early in radio broadcasting history in this country, the pioneering work of Guthrie and Sieveking in intrinsic *radio* drama showed clearly that the medium had possibilities well outside the business of merely reproducing in sound, plays specifically conceived for the theatre. Parallel with this growth, there had developed the cinema of fact (in distinction to fiction) which presently was to show its counterpart in terms of radio. With that unhappily over-abundant confusion of words so prevalent especially in all the temporal arts, a 'feature' in radio was the exact opposite of its counterpart in cinema: a radio 'feature' was the equivalent of a film 'documentary'. Grierson, always more of a teacher than an actual film-maker, had coined the word 'documentary' to indicate the nature of a form of cinema which fulfilled the O.E.D.'s definition of the word documentary itself: 'that which serves to show or prove something'. The factual radio feature programme — and the word applied equally to current and historical fact — and the documentary film are synonymous. Both forms

[97]

are necessarily by their very nature dramatic if the meaning of drama is conflict. With the advent of TV, the word 'feature', insofar as it applies to television and sound broadcasting, has dropped out of use. We still speak of 'feature' films but only in the sense of a film trade classification.

Documentary cinema and radio needed good writing, which in turn needed strong, imaginative interpretation in its presentation, just as drama and music in the theatre have always needed those essential elements. Auden and Dylan Thomas wrote commentaries for documentary films; MacNeice contributed to radio in the form of scripts *in toto*, eventually becoming, in some instances, interpreter of his own work, in that he directed that work himself. The Features Department of the BBC's Drama Division was originally initiated and led during the war years by Laurence Gilliam who, in the United Kingdom, may very roughly be said to have occupied in radio much the same position as Grierson did in documentary film. It was a large department and made a very substantial contribution to wartime radio broadcasting. MacNeice joined it as a script writer.

In 1941 the BBC was asked officially to make an appropriate gesture to our Soviet ally. It fell to my lot to put forward ideas for such a programme. I had long regarded Eisenstein's *Alexander Nevsky* as a milestone in the history of cinema, and certainly Eisenstein's greatest achievement up to that time. The BBC possessed a copy of the film as it had been used, at my instigation, by the engineering section of the early Television Service (1936-39) to introduce camera operators to the art of visual composition. In 1938 Prokofiev had made a cantata from the music he had originally composed for the film on Eisenstein's insistence. I asked MacNeice if he thought it possible to do a radio adaptation, using the Prokofiev score. He saw the film and undertook to have a shot at what in any event could be no more than a paraphrase. It was the first time I had worked with this intensely shy, seemingly aloof man and I found the collaboration exciting and rewarding. He wrote an excellent script, beautifully timed, and we proceeded to embark upon what was to be the most ambitious radio feature to date. The score and parts were obtained from Paris and as the work calls for very large orchestral and choral resources we decided to operate at Bedford where the Music Division was stationed, using the BBC Symphony Orchestra, BBC Chorus and BBC Theatre Chorus conducted by Sir Adrian Boult. The first performance took place on

9 December, 1941, the night after Pearl Harbour, with Robert Donat in the name part. MacNeice and I had persuaded the Soviet Ambassador (Maisky) to record an opening announcement; thus, the air-continuity on that memorable occasion was Roosevelt, Churchill, and then Maisky announcing the tribute to our ally. Apart from the high quality of MacNeice's writing, the magnificence of Donat's performance and the general excellence of the cast, orchestral playing and choral singing, the production was something of an advance technically. It was the first time such a programme had been done in an 'open' studio (in distinction to the multi-studio technique then common to features and drama) and a new film recording system had been put into action to record the work. It was a success. The Ministry of Information invited Donat to make a personal tour of the country's cinemas, his appearances concluding with his speaking the peroration from *Alexander Nevsky*, the last lines of which are:

> This is my message to every Russian
> And to all the Russians — to stand together.
> And this is my message to the rest of the world;
> We in Russia are children of peace,
> We do not envy any man's goods or country,
> And we do not close our doors to any peaceful visitor.
> I, Alexander Nevsky, speak on behalf of Russia
> And I say this to the rest of the world:
> If you will come to us in peace you are welcome,
> But if you come with the sword or the threat of the sword,
> Then remember the old saying —
> We proved it true once again yesterday,
> Proved it true on the frozen lake against the might of the
> Germans —
> "Those who take the sword
> By the sword shall they perish."

Many of MacNeice's big speeches speak better than they read; as a dramatist, therefore, actors were grateful to him and Donat was no exception. The success of *Alexander Nevsky* occasioned MacNeice and my being asked by the BBC to find a subject to celebrate the 450th anniversary of the discovery of America which fell on the 12th October of the next year — 1942. Thus, our second collaboration started almost immediately after *Nevsky's* first performance.

The life of Christopher Columbus is of enormous fascination as it involves almost every facet of the human condition and the consequence of the man's achievement, of course, is incalculable. MacNeice and I were fortunate in that having decided to tackle this canvas of epic size we had to hand a work which is now regarded by historians and scholars as being as definitive as is possible for the whole Columbus *mythos* ever to become. Samuel Eliot Morison's *Admiral of the Ocean Sea* (one of Columbus's actual titles demanded of Ferdinand and Isabella of Spain) is the *magnum opus* of a great historian and seaman. Morison's book not only covers every known aspect of Columbus's life in most scholarly detail but Morison has himself personally sailed all Columbus's courses. Our documentation, therefore, being so readily available, we set about taking full advantage of the fine opportunity the BBC had handsomely offered us. MacNeice's task in breaking down Morison's vast narrative into a manageable dramatic whole was formidable and in general I think he succeeded admirably. I was determined that the musical counterpart to MacNeice's text should match the letter in quality and I offered its composition to Walton whom I had been fortunate enough previously to introduce to the cinema. The result was an exceptionally fine score set to an excellent text. As in *Nevsky*, the resources needed were very large. I placed no restrictions on Walton whose requirements were comparable to those he used for his great cantata *Belshazzar's Feast*. The script called for thirty-two speaking parts and the cast, orchestra and chorus (again conducted by Boult) were set to operate in the huge 'open' studio represented by the Corn Exchange at Bedford. The first performance of *Christopher Columbus* took place on 12 October 1942, with Laurence Olivier in the name part and the production was repeated (it had been recorded as had *Nevsky* by the Phillips-Hill process) on 8 April 1973, as jointly part of the BBC 50th anniversary and of Walton's 70th birthday celebrations. Olivier gave a performance in *Christopher Columbus* of great weight and authority. MacNeice's sense of situation is very evident when he gives a soliloquy to Columbus who, in the full cycle of doubt and optimism, is somewhere in mid-Atlantic.

> Where shall wisdom be found and where is the abode of
> understanding?
> God makes the weight for his winds and he weigheth the waters
> by measure.

They knew that I was to come.
Isaiah and Esdras and Job and John the Divine —
They knew that I was to come.
And the Roman poet, Seneca, knew it too —
. . . venient annis
Saecula seris quibus oceanus
Vincula rerum laxet. . . .
"The time will come in a late
Century when the sea
Will loose the knots of fate
And the earth will be opened up
And the rolled map unfurled
And a new sailor sail
To uncover a new world."
"The time will come. . . ." The time has come already.
There are strange things happening.

The words in Olivier's voice, backed by Walton's music, add up to something magical.

My next and, alas, last collaboration with MacNeice was of a totally different nature. I had left the BBC, co-produced with Olivier the film of *Henry V* in 1944, and was engaged in preparing a major film concerning the future, and the future of peace in particular, with stress on the importance of aviation within that context. I invited MacNeice to write the dialogue. He had had no experience of cinema — which, of course, was of no moment whatsoever — and I was impressed and helped by his readiness to study and quickly to grasp the constructional quintessence of, for him, a new medium. *Pax Futura* was never produced — its costs would have been stratospheric — nor published. But a quote from a soliloquy given to Flavius, the leading male character, gives a measure of its style:

All these lives in my hands — and yet not in my hands.
If only I knew what this conspiracy is!
Beyond the general terms of the warning from Rio
And beyond my own intuition. Oh yes I know
The kind of thing that it is, I recognise from of old
The hydra heads reappearing — the anti-men
Who will never give up until they unmake, undo
What the craftsmen of peace and freedom have done and made.

Twenty years ago I prevented a world war
As a delegate from my nation — and since then as a servant
Of an international order I confined
Myself by choice to my job, have been a good executive
And always, as my father taught me, clung to —
Old-fashioned though it sounds — the ideal of Service,
Old Stoic that he was! I wonder if my mother
Had not died in childbirth — Service makes a full
Life in a way but women — Supposing Helen . . .
Flavius! Is this the time to be sentimental?
The anti-men are upon you — they want a verdict.
A verdict? Right. They shall have one.
I will speak a few words to my passengers.

TIME AND THE WILL
LIE SIDESTEPPED:
ATHENS, THE INTERVAL

KEVIN ANDREWS

I first saw him at a marble-staired reception, looking opaque.

Part of the academic curriculum of the foreign archaeological schools in Athens is, besides entertaining one another, to keep up with a handpicked — (choice determined in accordance with the regime currently in power) — section of the local intellectuals, government functionaries, gentry and heads of foreign Missions. Not the sort of gathering where one might have expected to meet Louis MacNeice. Nevertheless by one of those chance remarks that, even in the awful babble, set a condersation going and cement a friendship before it has yet, so to speak, happened, I found myself deep in talk with a handsome unknown redhaired lady who was clearly paying attention to what an insignificant student of mediaeval archaeology had to tell her about a flourishing detention-camp for political prisoners, called Makronisos. For Greeks the place was famous and, in certain circles, it was wiser not to speak of it, but in early 1950, with the Civil War barely at an end, it was only a few foreign visitors and international sub-committees with supposedly objective or perhaps philanthropic intentions that went there and usually chose to remain silent on what they had seen.

'Louis, come over here, this is interesting', and, after a few more vicarious heroics by me addressed to the straight and grace-ful husband with the expressionless look of someone either quite bored or quite receptive, that (amid the yelping and bared teeth and feathered hats) was that.

Until the occasion broke up and, having learned the identity of the famous poet whom I hadn't heard of, I — relentless literary snob — took care to reach the marble exit at the same time he did.

Something had clicked, and they took me home to dinner in the 'bland blank room like a doctor's consulting room / With its too many exits, all of glass and frosted' that had been rented for him as the newly arrived Director of the British Institute in Athens. Just as that title was a bit ponderous for him, so the flat, (Athenian-1930, like a hotel suite in Ankara), with its brown walls and sliding panels, and furnishings not positively ugly so much as absolutely tasteless, didn't look like his milieu, or hers.

'We haven't had time to make it look MacNeice-y,' said she, with the faintest hint of confident possession or recklessly clear purpose in which a reader of the future might have sensed a warning.

They soon became my closest friends in Athens, and we gravitated to each other again in New York and London in later years when life began to pinch and the issues out of difficulties to show signs of closing off successively. It was a curious friendship. He was seventeen years older than I. He had lived a life that I had only gazed at from a protected youth. He had completed the better part of a life's work already, where I had only a few pages in a drawer. He was illustrious where I had been brought up more to crave fame than do anything to acquire it. He had written some great poems, but it was long before I read any. Sometimes (that opaque expression!) I felt I was a nuisance dropping in so often. Most of the time he never talked, mostly looked past you at a world you didn't have a place in. So it was matter for astonishment that on two or three occasions he looked me in the eye, or read me a poem just completed, or talked to me in a warm and relaxed manner that I didn't know how to reciprocate, or even shrank away from — out of a perverse small fear that, if I stayed, he wouldn't. Once too from another room I watched him at a dining-table sitting up till 3.00 in the morning, trying to make suitable for publication a clumsy article I had written on returning from a mountain area in the grip of a guerrilla war. And once, when his son was in America, he wrote asking me to carry out an uncomfortable mission. But with all of this, spaced out over a period of twelve years I can hardly say I ever got to know him well. Either he was too polite, too decent, too considerate (the way former generations were) of someone else's privacy, or else he was mostly unable to come out from behind a kind of frosted glass inside himself; or perhaps it was just that, like any man with an attractive witty talented ebullient wife, it had become a habit with him to leave the business of communicability to her.

In the beginning the Greek surroundings were an integral and helpful part of the picture. We went for some good walks together: on Hydra before foreigners had heard of it, and on the mountains around Athens — which still looked like a French provincial town, where barely more than the occasional bus or taxi lumbered down the main thoroughfares — sometimes with their eight-year-old daughter and his teenage son on holiday from England (before *ce dernier* got himself subtracted from his father's life); and two whom I met at their place became my best friends later, which isn't doing badly.

They had a fearless instinct for getting the right people together, which sometimes meant the wrong people: ready at any time to mix the great with the small or the prominent with the forgotten, in such a way as to produce clashes, arguments and revelations one would have heard nowhere else. Once, for the sake of the world's greatest Hellenist, they pitted the Representative of British diplomacy in Greece against a leader of a Wartime Resistance that had been betrayed by Greece and England both; once again letting all hell get loose between the latter — perhaps the most brilliant man in Athens — and the Wartime architect of that foreign diplomacy, a man of equal intellect and courage, greater renown, less experience, and a more fortunate survival. Musicians, poets, painters — some not yet famous — were all to be met in the frosty brown flat, and only seldom the more prominent idiots of Athenian high society or London. It should be noted too that when his Athenian prominence first propelled MacNeice to read his poems publicly, his voice was harsh, grating, disagreeable; it was thanks largely to his wife that he learned to read his poems almost better than he wrote them.

At that time the British Institute existed to make available perhaps the only thing a bankrupt Britain had available for export, namely its culture, in a capital that, even after the promulgation of the Truman Doctrine in 1947, still considered itself an outpost of the Sterling Area but that, since 1940, had had little time for culture. The Institute was housed in a Neoclassical building at the corner of Kolonaki Square, graceful inside with gold-and-white Ionic columns, and it gave out a stream of concerts, song-recitals, what the MacNeices called their Double Act, poetry readings, lectures and plays, that all reflected the invention and imaginativeness of its director and his wife. The British Council was still something else, a drab building with a closed door one block off. A few months after Louis's arrival, Institute was merged with Council, for reasons of economy, by that Welfare State that he had hoped for, partly dreaded, still believed in. He became second in command; the boss was an ex-Eton housemaster who wore metal heels to his shoes that clicked. Boss and Assistant didn't like each other; they had communicating offices but, rather than use the door, restricted their communication to sending notes out through the corridor by messenger. The drab building was given up, and Louis became an administrator in the light and columned neo-classical house (now replaced by something six storeys high, in concrete with a tiny auditorium).

Something happened. Failed to happen. Eighteen months, and he never got really much involved in any Greek life outside the microscopic asphyxiating circle of the English-speaking Athenian Establishment. One summer spent in their maid's village at the wild rough end of one of the least known islands of the Aegean (from Byzantine times a place of exile, under the Metaxas dictatorship and again during the Civil War a place of enforced rustication for political prisoners), then a climb up Psiloríti and a few trips into the provinces — these were not enough to spark him off, though some of the prisoners on Ikaria were his contemporaries and most were to go on to places worse, and all had been fired by the same urge that had once sent so many volunteers, reporters and observers — including himself — to Spain.

A poem about this island in *Ten Burnt Offerings* contains one indifferent stanza about 'prisoners really, here in the hills,' and shows no attempt to recapture an old fervour or respond to a burning issue. He is more interested in himself. '. . . This middle stretch / Of life is bad for poets,' he states, with a lameness that reflects it. And 'Only my wits with nothing to grind on' is not altogether an excuse.

The ten long poems written during his first twelve months in Greece no doubt served to get his writing muscles working again. They contain (despite lines too clogged with consonants and concepts) plenty of ideas that it's a delight to go back to for decoding, as well as some inspired historical, mythological, geographical, psychological, and even religious writing, that lack however the immediacy and casual bite of *Autumn Journal*, Section XII, written twelve years earlier, after the Munich Agreement and his experience of Barcelona. In this the history, literature, philosophy and moral issues of ancient Greece were not only compressed into sixty-eight lines, but also fused into an epitaph for 1938. This kind of writing he was never to equal, though he did surpass it later with a leap-frog, as it were, past all historical or social or collective issues, back to the very origins of language and of English prosody, back to rhythms very old, yet showing a firmer grip than ever on the contemporary and devastating image, and now looking ahead (without the consolations of solidarity or dogma or belief in human progress) to the pressure-chamber of the final solitude and the empty place where Death and he would go for a walk together.

What does come through in *Ten Burnt Offerings* of the Greece of 1950-51 (strictly speaking, Athens, Missolonghi, Ikaria) is clearly secondary to the personal predicament of a man who has reached an age in life when promises give out, prove false, and there are no others coming. But this he wasn't facing yet, or not completely, and he was able to get by with a few ideas and descriptive images so apt as to recall Henry James's deadly injunction: 'Poetry should be at least as well written as prose.'

A pity he didn't penetrate more deeply into the place and time; only he could have done it justice. But he was twelve years older now. Nor was he galvanized by that wave of European feeling that made the Spanish Civil War the *cause célèbre* of the 1930s. In actual fact a civil war had been going on in Greece for longer than the war in Spain, but it was more confused and bedevilled as an issue. Not many outsiders — except of course the interested parties, and they mostly behind the scene — were informed about, or even interested in, the Resistance, the clashes and the trouble brewing between its separate bands, the December Uprising, the fierce plebiscite of 1946, and the horrors of 1947 on; the Cold War was bigger; after the atom bomb, Korea. To see the horrors inside Greece one had to look into the poorer quarters of Athens or outside it altogether, which he mostly didn't. The Athens he frequented had none of the atmosphere of Barcelona, where everyone had been in it. And in 1950 there was not much surface indication of what Athens was destined to turn into some twenty years later, when everyone would be in it too. . . . In 1950 he was a Man with a Job, in a place that was gasping for breath — his attention turned to work, responsibility, position, family, and the first cracks in the fabric of his living.

A tired time, a time of relaxation that, after a show of intricate analysis, could turn too easily to resignation. The first poems he had written in two years (I remember him walking down from Ghika's house on Hydra to the port, muttering all the way indistinguishable words) show certainly an appreciation of the touching or picturesque phenomena of Greece; nothing more, although one poem harks back to St. Paul and the Eumenides, and another to Byron and the myth of Meleager, and either poem is enough to contradict my quibbling.

And so one shouldn't talk too much. Yet I keep coming back to the impression he gave then of someone unresisting, which didn't later seem to be his style when one saw the caged beast inside him; and I would hazard the assertion that his time in Greece was a parenthesis, an emptiness, between the involved, erotic tragic years of the 'thirties and the blitz, and the booming, bitter, boozy life at the BBC before he died. It was possible to look out, with his unique lens, at surfaces conveniently impenetrable or back, with X-ray vision, to a past conveniently remote and perhaps comfortably dark (that he could light up with a few dazzling gymnastics) but quite, I think, impossible for him to look too closely at the curious exhausted age that precedes the age of more acute despair.

There's little one can say about a gap — whether in a life, a sentence, or an *oeuvre* — except that it may coincide with a time when inaction, or just breathing-space, is vital.

And so, at his Athenian post, with wit and grace and diligence discharging British functions and representing the cultural heritage of the English language, there was something just a bit anomalous about a man incapable of representing anything except himself — whatever that might be.

Knowing him then, it was difficult to visualize him as the subject of a Ph.D. thesis. His place in the World of Letters is important and will become more so, but the ideal biography of him would be a fearless, absolutely intimate and dense-knit study of a life, and of the lives it touched, and of the history of Europe in his time, and of his success and failure as a poet.

Poets who don't go on writing their best poems all the time cause irritation to the public. This isn't fair. Still, without the injudicious untalented and envious public to carp at its less even poets, these would be lost. Poets are human beings. The human being is more interesting than the poet *qua* dictionary definition, deriving from the Greek for 'maker' — eternal busybody who can leave nothing alone, that pain-in-the-arse with a chip on his shoulder or club on his foot, calling through an endless night for somebody to pay attention and (dead friend, forgive me) 'lament for the Makers'.

Quite vain, this one: no more than you or I however. Modest to an unusual degree. Childishly happy over a piece of work accomplished, a new book out. Grim over intimations of failure, boredom or advancing age. I don't know what the word is, but the opposite of pompous. Though he had taught Greek at Birmingham and English at Cornell, he would never have turned poet on Campus. No mantle of official dignity stood a chance of settling on his shoulders, though he was one of the high-ups at the BBC and got the C.B.E. and once directed a cultural institution in a little capital that demands, craves any kind of literary or academic grandeur (a title will do at a pinch) from any dignitary representing Britain, great or small.

A short life ripening steadily. A radiant life, with plenty of ambiguous or murky patches. A man not altogether admirable or kind. Someone profoundly frightened, therefore modern. Able to live with fear, and therefore classical. Able to exhaust his greatest talent, his involvement (like a compass-needle) in the history being lived around him. Although certain poems in *The Burning Perch* and the last manuscript poem 'Thalassa' are certainly among the most intimately tragic ever written, he was able to write dull poems as well as miracles, and in the autobiographical fragment, perhaps the finest and most honest prose of the century. Someone too conscientious at his jobs, too careless of himself, perhaps too generous. Far-seeing to a fatal point. Too erudite, intelligent, distinguished. Yet once he socked Roy Campbell on the jaw and once he wrenched his wife out of an upper berth on the Irish mail boat and threw her on the floor. A man who lost things: a mother when he was five, a wife and then a son, then his connection to another wife, and then his life for no reason whatsoever. Someone withdrawn and very difficult to reach, who would sometimes startle you by showing you he had been there all the time.

FOR LOUIS MACNEICE

ANTHONY THWAITE

Your long face, like a camel's, swivels round
The long bar of the George, and stops at me
Coming in like bad news. The BBC
Recruits young graduates to rescue Sound
From all that bright-lit, show-biz sort of stuff
And I am one of them, arrived too late
For the Golden Age (the exact date
October Fifty-Seven), though enough
Remains like a penumbra of great days
To sanctify our efforts. There you stand
Aloof and quizzical, the long bar scanned
For friends or enemies, a scornful phrase
Poised to put down the parasite or bore;
But underneath that mask a lonely man
Looks out, lugubrious comedian
Or elegiac dandy, more and more
Driven into the corners of yourself.
Uncertain of your mood, after an hour
Of a shared office going slowly sour
With cigarettes and hangovers, the shelf
Above your desk capsizing with its load
Of scripts that date back sixteen years or more,
I try the Twickenham ploy, the sort of war
You relish, England-Ireland, worth an ode
Better than J. C. Squire tried long ago.
That does it. You prefer such stuff to bleak
Intensities of bookishness, and speak
With passion of who scored, and how, and know
Each quiddity of form and style and skill.
And yet I play this game only to thaw
That icy stare, because I'm still in awe
Of your most private self, that self you spill
Into the poems you keep locked away.

Looked back on now, how much I must despise
That Boswell-type with deferential eyes
Who saw you as a lion on display!
The living man eluded me. Though praise
Bitten out from those pursed, laconic lips
Astonished me, dismissal could eclipse
My universe for hours, even days.
Now that you're dead, I read you and I hear
Your nasal, almost strangled voice recite
Poems you wrote in loneliness at night,
Far from the George and parasites and beer.
My glum prosaic homage comes too late,
Ten years too late, for your embarrassment,
And yet those truant hours spent and mis-spent
Off Portland Place I humbly dedicate
To a Muse who watches, listens, is aware
Of every sell-out, every careless word,
Each compromise, each syllable that's blurred
With vanity or sloth, and whose blank stare
Chills and unmasks me as yours used to do.
Forgive me, Louis, for such well-meant verse,
Such running-on where you would have been terse,
And take the thanks I meant to give to you.

MACNEICE IN ENGLAND
AND IRELAND

DEREK MAHON

The time is coming fast, if it isn't already here, when the question, 'Is So-and-So really an *Irish* writer?' will clear a room in seconds. Was Kafka a Czech writer or a German one? Picasso a Spanish painter or a French one? These questions are interesting up to a point, but there is no need to find answers to them. Was Yeats, after all, an Irish poet or an English one? The answer is, both. He was an Irishman who took part in the London literary life of his day, and is widely considered to be the greatest English poet of the twentieth century. The question is semantic, and not important except in so far as the writer himself makes it so. Reading through the *Collected Poems* of Louis MacNeice one notices that, in purely quantitative terms, there is not a great deal specifically about Ireland. The same is true of Beckett. Yet it would take a lot of obtuseness to deny that some sort of Irish sensibility is frequently discernible in the work of both. A mordancy perhaps, and a fascination with the fact of language itself, deriving from an inherited sense of the lethal possibilities of words:

> Natives of poverty, children of malheur,
> The gaiety of language is our seigneur.

The English public school system has a way of ironing out regional, and indeed national differences, and turning its products into Englishmen; and this is what happened to MacNeice. As a small boy he was sent to a prep school in Dorset, later went on to Marlborough, and finished his formal education at Oxford. Afterwards he worked in English universities, the BBC and the British Council, all of which made him a fully paid-up member of the British academic, artistic and administrative Establishment. His contemporaries were not Frank O'Connor, Denis Johnston and Patrick Kavanagh, but Cyril Connolly, Noel Coward and William Empson. He had no place in the intellectual history of modern

Ireland: his place was in Oxford, Hampstead or Broadcasting House, among Englishmen who had had the same sort of education as himself. Nor was he an outsider. I once overheard, in Trinity College, Dublin, an exchange between two flaxen-haired youths of the *Horse and Hound* variety: 'I say, are you English?' 'Neao.' 'Neither am I.' Remove the element of caricature (his voice retained traces of a Northern snarl, and his manner a certain taciturnity, to the end of his days) and there you have, socially speaking, the extent of MacNeice's Irishness.

Similarly, his poetry is of largely English derivation. His education, like Rupert Brooke's, was Classical, Anglo-Hellenic. The poets he most admired were Chaucer, Dryden, Keats, Hardy, and the casualties of the trenches: Edward Thomas, Wilfred Owen. Only an 'English' poet could have written:

> The patch
> Of sky at the end of the path grows and discloses
> An ordered open air long ruled by dyke and fence,
> With geese whose form and gait proclaim their consequence,
> Pargetted outposts, windows browed with thatch,
> And cow pats — and inconsequent wild roses.
>
> ('Woods')

I think it extremely unlikely that he was on close terms with any Irish poet, except his fellow-Ulsterman, W. R. Rodgers. He met Yeats, briefly, with E. R. Dodds, in the 1930s, and later wrote a book about him; but there is no evidence that he was ever 'influenced' by him. His account of the meeting is rather dry, in fact: 'He talked a great deal about the spirits. "Have you ever seen them?" Dodds asked (Dodds could never keep back such questions). Yeats was a little piqued. No, he said grudgingly, he had never actually seen them . . . but — with a flash of triumph — he had often *smelt* them.' MacNeice was on holiday in Ireland when Britain declared war on Germany; and here, remembering his own passionate interest in the public events of his time, we must read between the lines: '. . . spent Saturday drinking in a bar with the Dublin literati; they hardly mentioned the war but debated the correct versions of Dublin street songs. . . .'

There have been several attempts, notably by W. T. McKinnon in *Apollo's Blended Dream*, to upgrade MacNeice from minor poet to major. He was, says McKinnon, a philosophical poet of unsuspected depth, one who struggled through life to reach a higher synthesis of sense and spirit. The argument is persuasive and often illuminating, but the conventional estimate of his achievement is probably here to stay. Ian Hamilton, in his *Poetry Chronicle*, warns us not to be too solemn about a poet 'who loved the surface but lacked the core'. But Hamilton misses the point, I think. For Mac-Neice, as for Wallace Stevens, the surface *was* the core. Like Horace, he was *profoundly* superficial.

The poems that made his name in the 1930's are the ones where the love of surface is most in evidence, culminating in *Autumn Journal*, which provides the most extraordinary visual and tactile sense of the period outside the early novels of Graham Greene. If Dublin could be reconstructed from the pages of *Ulysses*, as Joyce claimed, the pre-war urban England of rainy tramlines, Corner Houses, Bisto Kids and Guinness Is Good For You could probably be roughly simulated from a reading of Greene and MacNeice. Compare the opening of *England Made Me*:

> She might have been waiting for her lover. For half an hour she had sat on the same high stool, half turned from the counter, watching the swing door. Behind her the ham sandwiches were piled under a glass dome, the urns gently steamed. As the door swung open, the smoke of engines silted in, grit on the skin and like copper on the tongue.
>
> 'Another gin.' It was her third. Damn him, she thought with tenderness, I'm hungry. . . .

with this, from *Autumn Journal*:

> Nelson is stone and Johnnie Walker moves his
>   Legs like a cretin over Trafalgar Square.
> And in the Corner House the carpet-sweepers
>   Advance between the tables after crumbs. . . .
>
> And I feel a certain pleasurable nostalgia
>   In sitting alone, drinking, wondering if you
> Will suddenly thread your way among these vulcanite tables
>   To a mutually unsuspected rendezvous.

Was he the first English poet to make habitual use of brand names? It seems likely. At a time when the British documentary cinema was at its most accomplished, in the days of John Grierson and Alexander Korda, when Auden scripted *Night Mail* and Isherwood *I Am a Camera*, and Greene wrote film criticism for *The Spectator*, there was nothing bizarre in the notion of poetry-as-documentary; and this is where MacNeice excelled. He might even be said to have invented the genre. So far as the British reading public is concerned, it's probably what he will be remembered for. The Irish reading public will be looking for other things.

MacNeice, like most of his generation, was intensely interested in world events. Though not 'political' like Spender and Day Lewis, who joined (for a time) the Communist Party, or like Orwell, who fought in Spain, he shared the generalised left-wing sympathies of his Oxford and Cambridge contemporaries. Poets, he said, should read the newspapers and know something about economics. Although a non-combatant, he visited Spain and wrote poems about it. The European poets he admired, and sometimes translated, were 'committed' figures like Brecht, Aragon and Paul Eluard. He was apprehensive about the rise of Fascism, conventionally dubious about Communism, hostile to capitalism, and indifferent to formal religion — the very model, in fact, of a liberal intellectual. What did he make of Ireland in political terms? His dislike of the Unionist hegemony in the North was unqualified. Where did his sympathies lie? Beckett, asked to contribute to a symposium on the Spanish Civil War, replied with a one-word telegram: 'UPTHEREPUBLIC'. MacNeice, too, was anti-Franco, as was consistent with his agnostic, mildly socialist position. Not everyone was. In England, Catholic Tories like Evelyn Waugh and literary bully-boys like Roy Campbell supported the Nationalists; while in Ireland more supported them than not. (One well-known writer took the trouble to declare himself neutral.) Frank Ryan and others like him who joined the International Brigade were the exception rather than the rule in Ireland where respectable opinion was more concerned with the perpetuation of Christ's Kingdom on Earth than with the survival of the Spanish Republic. My guess is that MacNeice was conscious of this and that it served to reinforce his doubts about Ireland — doubts which were further reinforced by Irish neutrality during the Second World War. His attitude to the place had always been characterized by a certain impatience:

Your drums and your dolled-up Virgins and your ignorant dead.
('Valediction')

Increasingly, his view of Official Ireland (the Ireland of patriotic graft and pious baloney) was one of positive distaste, which is all right coming from Austin Clarke but bad manners from a Northern Protestant. There is a belief, prevalent since the time of Thomas Davis, that Irish poetry, to be Irish, must somehow express the National Aspirations; and MacNeice's failure to do so (the National Aspirations, after all, include patriotic graft and pious baloney) is one of the reasons for his final exclusion from the charmed circle, known and feared the world over, of Irish Poets. 'A tourist in his own country', it has been said, with the implication that this is somehow discreditable. But of what sensitive person is the same not true? The phrase might stand, indeed, as an epitaph for Modern Man, beside Camus's 'He made love and read the newspapers.'

MacNeice spent quite a lot of time in Ireland, but always on some sort of holiday — to stay in rented cottages in North Antrim, Donegal or Connemara; to visit the artists George and Mercy McCann in Belfast; or to watch international rugby matches at Lansdowne Road. In 1938 he applied, unsuccessfully, for the Chair of English at Trinity. It was the nearest he ever came to living in Dublin:

> This was never my town,
> I was not born nor bred
> Nor schooled here and she will not
> Have me alive or dead.
> ('The Closing Album, I')

(Alive, no. Dead, you can make what you like of him.) There are several attempts in the early poems to establish an Irish persona, but none is very convincing. Ryan, in 'Eclogue from Iceland', describes himself as an 'exile', but there is a measure of disingenuousness here. 'Exile', in the histrionic and approximate sense in which the word is used in Ireland, was an option available to Joyce and O'Casey, who 'belonged' to the people from whom they wished to escape. It was not available, in the same sense, to MacNeice, whose background was a mixture of Anglo-Irish and Ulster Protestant (C. of I.). Whatever his sympathies he didn't, by class or religious background, 'belong to the people'. How then, not sharing the general constraints, could he free himself from them? He had known the freedom of privilege from childhood on:

> I was the rector's son, born to the anglican order,
>   Banned for ever from the candles of the Irish poor.
> .   .   .   .
> I went to school in Dorset, the world of parents
>   Contracted into a puppet world of sons,
> Far from the mill girls, the smell of porter, the salt mines
>   And the soldiers with their guns.
>
> ('Carrickfergus')

Even so, Irish landscapes and preoccupations crop up continually at every stage of his development. If 'Valediction', written at the age of twenty-six, represents a formal anticipation of his non-Irish future, the final closing of a door which had opened only as a provisional possibility:

> Therefore I resign, good-bye the chequered and the quiet hills
> The gaudily-striped Atlantic, the linen-mills
> That swallow the shawled file, the black moor where half
> A turf-stack stands like a ruined cenotaph.
>
> ('Valediction')

there was still 'memory in apostasy' — the frequent, Proustian reversion to the images and circumstances of childhood:

> Surprises keep us living; as when the first light
> Surprised our infant eyes or as when, very small,
> Clutching our parents' hands we toddled down a road
> Where all was blank and windless both to touch and sight
> Had we not suddenly raised our eyes which showed
> The long grass blowing wild on top of the high wall.
>
> ('Mutations')

The idea of 'surprise' is central to MacNeice's work. It is closely linked to his love of sensation and to that profound superficiality which is really a version of the empirical humanism which lies at the heart of his poetry. Consider 'Train to Dublin':

> I give you the smell of Norman stone, the squelch
> Of bog beneath your boots, the red bog-grass,
> The vivid chequer of the Antrim hills, the trough of dark
> Golden water for the cart-horses, the brass
> Belt of serene sun upon the lough.

And I give you the faces, not the permanent masks,
But the faces balanced in the toppling wave —
His glint of joy in cunning as the farmer asks
Twenty per cent too much, or a girl's, forgetting to be suave,
A tiro choosing stuffs, preferring mauve.

This is the first of many similar formulations, and a key to the 'Irishness' of his work. This 'tourist in his own country' enjoyed, as a tourist should, the sensuous qualities of light and landscape, for both of which he had a painter's eye — Paul Henry's perhaps, but a painter's even so. Note, however, the association of ideas. Variety and vividness of landscape immediately suggest the variety and vividness of human personality and experience. Nothing in his poetry carries such conviction and delight as the continual rediscovery of this equation in its many forms. The landscape can be a fashionable cocktail bar or a provincial tea-shop, a concert or a football match, a cottage fireside or a London street on the morning after an air-raid. The situation may be dramatic or banal. But what MacNeice latches onto is the existential tingle of the passing minute:

> Whether the living river
> Began in bog or lake,
> The world is what was given,
> The world is what we make
> And we only can discover
> Life in the life we make.
> ('London Rain')

It follows that his heroes are discoverers of 'life in the life we make'. He had no *literary* heroes: his love, there, was for the impersonal and remote, for Nietzsche and the Greek tragedians. His heroes, like Yeats's, were his friends. They appear in the poems, under their own names or under pseudonyms. Gwilym, in *Autumn Sequel*, is clearly recognisable as Dylan Thomas. Maguire, in the same poem, is George McCann, who also appears in *The Strings are False*:

> Back in the North there was a painter too whom I saw, George McCann, who had done surrealist work but thought most surrealists were phoney. George, like George the electrician in Birmingham, was a man who suited the name — you couldn't imagine him having any other. He had the rich

earthy quality, shot with grains of humour, that every George should have. I used to spend weekends in his cottage in Co. Armagh, drinking whiskey and exchanging our memories of the ludicrous, then sleeping on the floor by a turf fire. . . .

Another friend, perhaps his oldest and closest, was Graham Shepard, with whom he had been at school and who was to die at sea while serving with the Royal Navy in the Atlantic during the war. MacNeice's epitaph for Shepard, 'The Casualty', is one of my own favourites. This fine, stately elegy, distantly reminiscent of 'Lycidas' — the youthful friendship, the death at sea, the promise unfulfilled — but without the coldness of 'Lycidas', contains, in its pen-portrait of the dead man, the essence of MacNeice's empirical humanism:

> For you were a good mixer and could laugh
> With Rowlandson or Goya and you liked
> Bijoux and long-eared dogs and silken legs
> And titivated rooms but more than half
> Your story lay outside beyond the spiked
> Railing where in the night some old blind minstrel begs.

MacNeice contemplated with dismay the triumph of Mammon, the elevation of material smugness and spiritual ungenerosity at the expense of 'surprise'. Simplicity, warmth, 'the drunkenness of things being various', seemed to him to be threatened by a new Dark Age. Sometimes, during the 1930s, this is an image of the Thousand-Year Reich:

> We shall go down like palaeolithic man
> Before some new Ice Age or Genghiz Khan.
>   ('An Eclogue for Christmas')

More often it is a generalised evocation of a mean, denatured future, sharing some of the features of the consumer society ('The little sardine men crammed in a monster toy') and, oddly enough for someone sympathetic to socialism, of the Welfare State:

> Contraptions in ear or mouth or vagina
>
>   .   .   .   .
>
>   Assist yet degrade a generation
> For whom quality has long been in pawn to security.
>   ('Memoranda to Horace')

Against the advance of the 'monster toy' he deployed an imagery of warmth and growth, a rhetoric of irony and, increasingly, of nostalgia. It must have been clear to him, in his last years, that the things he valued were being daily outnumbered by the things he feared. Trying, for example, to find a seat in a renovated London pub throbbing with pop music can't have been much fun:

> To opt out now seems better than capitulate
> To the too-well-lighted and over-advertised
> Idols of the age. Sooner these crepuscular
>
> Blasphemous and bawdy exchanges; and even
> A second childhood remembering only
> Childhood seems better than a blank posterity,
> One's life restricted to standing room only.
>
> ('Memoranda to Horace')

These 'blasphemous and bawdy exchanges' are the province of the 'timeless vagrant' he mentions elsewhere and who resembles the 'old blind minstrel' in the elegy for Graham Shepard. Like Yeats he identifies this figure with Homer and Raftery. Perhaps he is Lazarus too, and Tiresias, and John the Baptist. Whoever he is, he is not an Englishman. His demeanour is of a kind for which there is no provision in the bland and temperate, the busy and practical, English tradition; nor has his authority to curse the great a precedent in English poetic practice. And yet, after all, his appearance here is rather self-consciously literary. MacNeice knew his Homer in the original, it goes without saying; but he can't have known more than a word or two of the language of Raftery. His allusion, then, is a wish-fulfilment, in its Homeric dimension a philhellenic dream of

> the misty West
> Remembered out of Homer but now yours.
>
> ('The Casualty')

The Islands of the Blest, the Hesperides, Tir na nOg, the Land of the Ever Young — call it what you will, it crops up regularly in MacNeice's poetry and is usually associated with the West of Ireland. Although he was born in Belfast, his father and grand-fathers before him grew up in the West of Ireland and MacNeice cultivated the fact as a private romance. (Also because 'It gives us a hold on the sentimental English.') But reality lay elsewhere, in an Ulster childhood and a life's work abroad:

> And the pre-natal mountain is far away.
> ('Carrick Revisited')

DESPAIR AND DELIGHT

JOHN MONTAGUE

When the *Collected Poems* of Louis MacNeice appeared, a strange thing happened. For years he had been taken for granted, even discounted; 'your verse half rubbish' as a minscule contemporary avers. He was never distant like Auden, a menacing intelligence, but easily met in bars, whether the George after a BBC recording, or over in Ireland for a rugby match. Like everyone else who knew him slightly, I cherish a few of those occasions. Once, driving to Lansdowne Road for a match through a thick throng of supporters, he spied a small man hurrying towards us against the stream. A languid finger followed his ducking progress: 'Must be an Ulster Catholic' said that rasping, intelligent voice — this for my benefit. It seemed to count more for him that I came from Tyrone, than that I wrote poetry; a childhood servant he had loved had come from there and names like Clogher and Augher and Fivemiletown had talismanic value for him. Used to the meanness of the Dublin literary scene, I found him disinterested, except in the serious sports of drinking and story telling, those frail rope-ladders across the void.

When he spoke of Auden, for example, it was not as a rival, but an admired friend, many of whose attitudes he could not accept. Taciturn himself, he loved word spinners like Thomas and Rodgers, a Presbyterian gone wild. He was inclined to speak deprecatingly of his own work, and when I told him that Tom Kinsella had been reading *Autumn Sequel*, he said: 'I suppose he found it less good than *Autumn Journal*, like everyone else.' He was pleased to hear the reverse, but I had the impression of someone who was resigned to being partially misunderstood, but content to follow out his path. Eminently approachable but ultimately lonely, he was delighted to meet anyone who had shared a milestone with him, especially in another life. In the 'Writers Workshop' at Iowa, where we first met, we discussed Dublin; in London we discussed the North from which we both came, the France where I was living, and where he hoped to come, for some kind of mythical holiday, away from the

established pattern of his life. Only in parts of Ireland did he seem
to dissolve into the warm bath of the present where myth and
moment meet:

> Both myth and seismic history have been long suppressed
> Which made and unmade Hy Brasil — now an image
> For those who despise charts but find their dream's endorsement
> In certain long low islets snouting towards the west
> Like cubs that have lost their mother.
>
> ('Last Before America')

And yet when he died, one's whole impression of him was
shocked back into recognition. Other poets like Roethke and Berry-
man, had passed through openly dialoguing with eternity, in their
theatrical American way. But Louis was so casual, made so little
attempt to involve us in his drama in the public sense, that the
melancholy premonitions of *The Burning Perch* did not strike home
until he had borne them out in his own death. In 'Goodbye to
London', a lover of life says goodbye to the urban life which had
sustained him, in 'The Introduction' to the love that had warmed
him, in 'The Suicide' to the office which had supported him, in
'Sports Page' to the games that had amused him. And the lurking
terror in his vision emerges as a reversal of the Christian promise:

> In lieu therefore of choice
> Thy Will be undone just as flowers
> Fugues, vows and hopes are undone. . . .
>
> ('In Lieu')

So, stunned, one reads back, to rediscover what had always been
there, under the bright plumage of his language, his professional
pride in his facility, in keeping the show going. MacNeice is one
of those whom melancholy had marked for her own; it had something to do with childhood and is present in the earliest poems.
'The candle in his white grave-clothes' and 'The dark blood of
night-time', to take phrases from two adjacent poems, come together
in those haunted nursery poems like 'Intimations of Mortality':

> Then the final darkness for eight hours
> The murderous grin of toothy flowers,
> The tick of his pulse in the pillow, the sick
> Vertigo of falling in a fanged pit.

And in 'Autobiography' we learn the age at which 'The little boy cannot go to sleep'.

> When I was five the black dreams came;
> Nothing after was quite the same . . .
>
> When my silent terror cried,
> Nobody, nobody replied.

Reading between the lines of his tight-lipped autobiography, a kind of early middle-aged exercise in personal therapy, one guesses that it has something to do with the mother, and the mongoloid brother. The latter is never mentioned in the poetry, but the mother is, in that strange poem 'Eclogue Between the Motherless', where her memory is what has to be exorcised:

> I thought 'Can I find a love beyond the family
> And feed her to the bed my mother died in. . . .'

And he associates his mother with that early boyhood anguish:

> Talking of ice
> I remembered my mother standing against the sky
> And saying "Go back in the house and change your shoes"
> And I kept having dreams and kept going back in the house.
> A sense of guilt like a scent — The day I was born
> I suppose that that same hour was full of her screams. . . .

We must accept that MacNeice is a poet of nightmare, only briefly allayed by love, or companionship. He has written a handful of the best love lyrics of our time, but they are also testimonies to the power of time to efface love. Love, indeed, can only exist outside time:

> Time was away and she was here
> And life no longer what it was. . . .

But 'Life will have her answer'; there is no lasting escape from the tedium and the terror. The best and bravest are those who can out-talk the monster: in Dylan Thomas, MacNeice recognised a fellow conspirator, possessed by, but defying death, 'he dared the passing bell / To pass him and it did'. The profound affection of Louis for anyone who could pass the time, anyone who could spin a web of words that transformed the dull earth into a magical place, even for the moment, shows in his splendid elegy for Dylan in *Autumn Sequel*.

> And so he cut his steps in the ice and rhymed
> His way up slowly, slowly by a star,
> While in his ears the bells of childhood chimed
>
> And avalanches roared beneath him far
> And the Three Kings went with him and the Three
> Gold Shoemakers of Wales, who would not mar
>
> A single stitch on a shoe, no more than he
> Would botch a verse. He made his own sea-shells
> In which to hear the voice of the sea,
>
> And knew the oldest creatures, the owl that tells
> How it has seen three forests rise and fall,
> And the great fish that plumbs the deepest wells. . . .

The enemy is time and Louis dealt with it in two ways. In his early work he is excited by the details of living, circuses, Christmas shopping, driving at night, travel, anything which illuminates the ordinary, and shows that 'world is suddener than we fancy it'. This is the great attraction of *Autumn Journal*, which is a catalogue of the pleasures of being alive, even 'in an evil time'. The philosophy behind this attitude, a determination to keep going, to keep alive, in the best sense, is summed up in another poem:

> And I would praise our inconceivable stamina
> Who work to the clock and calendar and maintain
> The equilibrium of nerves and notions,
> Our mild bravado in the face of time.
>
> ('Hidden Ice')

But 'Hidden Ice' finishes by reminding us that many end in suicide and madness, despite their daily disciplines. And in his middle years, when MacNeice abjured 'the velvet image' and 'the lilting measure' the enemy appears as repetition, boring and meaningless, a Parrot mouthing a catalogue which had once been a litany of fresh delights.

The cage is ungilded, the Parrot is loose on the world
Clapping his trap with gay but meaningless wings.

(Autumn Sequel)

Hence his affection for anyone who could, like Thomas, 'throw the
Parrot's lie / Back in its beak' and he links him with F. R. Higgins
(Reilly), an Irish poet from MacNeice's ancestral background of
Connaught:

and brown bogwater and blue

Hills followed him through Dublin with the same
Aura of knowing innocence, of earth
That is alchemized by light. . . .

(Autumn Sequel)

His Irish background is relevant because it corresponds to the two
facets of his vision. Ulster was the setting for his early melancholy
and may even have enhanced it: think of the language in the first
three stanzas of 'Carrickfergus' — 'lost sirens', 'the blind and halt',
'funeral cry', 'a drowning moon'. And the West from which his
father came, and to which Louis often returned on holiday, was
his favourite fantasy landscape, 'his dream's endorsement'.

. . . my mother
Earth was a rocky earth with breasts uncovered
To suckle solitary intellects. . . .

('Western Landscape')

And in the end it may have been an Irish quality, his easygoing
character, which prevented him from being as implacable in pessim-
ism as his great predecessor, Thomas Hardy. For it is in the
company of that great master of melancholy that I would finally
place him; the advocates of a lesser English tradition, linking
Hardy to Larkin, seem to forget MacNeice. *The Burning Perch,*
full of the sadness of an anticipated death, brings us back to the
lonely sadness of the early poems, a melancholy only briefly
vanquished by companionship and love. Under the delight that
glitters on the surface, there is always the hidden ice.

LOUIS MACNEICE

LIAM MILLER

For me, as for many of my generation, Louis was, first, the poet of 'Bagpipe Music', a piece which was one of the pointers to a correction in my thinking on poetry as conditioned by the set pieces for the Leaving Certificate of the 'thirties and 'forties. This was almost a decade before I decided to go into the poetry business as publisher, and almost two before I met the poet. My friendship with Louis was confined to his last years as it was, I think, late in 1959, when I was in London seeking an outlet through London Publishers for the work of the Dolmen Press, that I was introduced to Louis in the George. Here on visits to London I met Bertie Rodgers and Harry Craig and Jack MacGowran who had worked in theatre with me in Dublin years before. Here the tall quiet man questioned me about goings-on in Dublin, and I came to love our conversations which revealed how much, despite long years spent away from Ireland, he remained in touch with the Irish matters from which he drew so many themes in his work. And, too, how much encouragement he offered in my attempt to make our efforts known abroad.

Louis had given his 'Irish' poems to the Cuala Press for the book entitled *The Last Ditch* which appeared in 1940, and in September 1948 he came to Ireland for the burial of Yeats at Drumcliff. He came again in 1962 to honour Joyce at the dedication of the Tower at Sandycove. Then, after the ceremony and excitement we spent a quiet Sunday talking about the Irish poets, especially Austin Clarke, whose plays were going through the press and who, like Louis, drew on the day-to-day happenings of his world for many of his poems. Both poets, too, were pioneers in the revival of the poetic theatre — Louis in London on stage as well as over the radio, Austin through his Lyric Theatre productions in Dublin.

Louis MacNeice was one of the few modern poets included in the great exhibition covering six centuries of poetry in English presented by the National Book League in London in 1947. He is typical of the Anglo-Irish contribution to English literature and so

[129]

it was fitting that his last Irish journey should be to Carrowdore graveyard, as near the sea on the north-east Irish coast as Drumcliff is on the west, and where he lies buried beside the Bishop, his father in the Irish landscape which had been the setting for so many of his poetic adventures.

In 1966 I was offered his last play, *One for the Grave*, for production at our little theatre, the Lantern in Dublin, but we had not the resources necessary to stage the piece, so it became the first new play presented at the rebuilt Abbey Theatre in the Autumn of 1966. I designed the settings, among them a cloth based on Leonardo's Renaissance man — an echo of my feeling about this great Irish creative being who, in the application of his Irishness made it universal, and who, in restating the medieval *Everyman* within the framework of a twentieth-century television studio pointed a lesson in the eternal values that informed all his explorations in literature.

And again last year, for the tenth anniversary of Louis's death I had the opportunity to present a reading of his poems in Dublin in which I tried to affirm those qualities in his real monument, his work, which reflect those I found in a brief friendship with the man.

BOOKS WRITTEN
BY LOUIS MAC NEICE:
A CHECKLIST

CHRISTOPHER M. ARMITAGE

In the descriptions, the term 'American edition' means that the book was manufactured in the U.S.A.; the term 'American issue' means that the book was manufactured in Great Britain for sale in the U.S.A. under the imprint of an American publisher. Where ascertainable, the number of copies printed is cited; the number applies to the first impression only, unless stated otherwise.

1   BLIND FIREWORKS. Louis MacNeice. London: Victor Gollancz, 1929.
     Poems. First edition, 8vo, pp. (4), 80. Black cloth boards labelled on spine. 1,000 copies printed.

2   ROUNDABOUT WAY. Louis Malone [pseudonym]. Putnam, London & New York (1932).
     Novel. First edition, 8vo, pp. (8), 272. Blue cloth boards lettered in gold on spine.

3   POEMS. Louis MacNeice. London: Faber & Faber (1935).
     Poems. First edition, 8vo, pp. 68. Orange cloth boards lettered in gold on spine. 6,691 copies printed.

4   THE AGAMEMNON OF AESCHYLUS translated by Louis MacNeice. London: Faber & Faber (1936).
     Verse play in translation. First edition, 8vo, pp. (6), 72. Violet cloth boards lettered in gold on spine. 2,000 copies printed.

4a   ——— American issue. New York: Harcourt, Brace & Company (1937).
     Printed in Great Britain and identical with No. 4 except for beige cloth boards lettered in black. 260 copies printed.

4b ———— Re-issue. London: Faber paper covered Edition (1967).
Identical with No. 4 except in binding. 6,000 copies printed.

5 OUT OF THE PICTURE a play in two acts by Louis Mac-Neice. London: Faber & Faber (1937).
Play in verse and prose. First edition, 8vo, pp. (4), 128. Beige cloth boards lettered in blue on spine. 3040 copies printed.

5a ———— American issue. New York: Harcourt, Brace and Company (1938).
Printed in Great Britain and identical with No. 5 except for title page and blue cloth boards, labelled on spine. 520 copies printed.

6 LETTERS FROM ICELAND. W. H. Auden and Louis MacNeice. London: Faber & Faber (1937).
Poems and prose. First edition, 8vo, pp. 272, plus 31 pp. of photographs. Green cloth boards lettered in red and blue on spine. 10,269 copies printed. MacNeice contributed Chapters III, X, XII, XV, parts of XVII, and the Epilogue.

6a ———— First American edition. New York: Random House (1937).
Manufactured in U.S.A. Pagination as in No. 6, but pages of photographs interspersed more regularly. Beige cloth boards labelled on spine and front; some copies with grey boards. 3,000 copies printed.

6b ———— Re-issue. London: Faber paper covered Edition (1967).
Like No. 6, but the pages of photographs and Chapter XVI omitted : hence only 256 pp. 8,000 copies printed.

6c ———— Second American edition. New York: Random House (1969).
Manufactured in U.S.A. by the Book Press, Brattleboro, Vermont. Pp. 256, gathered in 16's. Black cloth boards, partially covered with blue paper, lettered in silver on spine. 3,000 copies printed.

7 POEMS by Louis MacNeice. New York: Random House (1937).
Poems. First edition, 8vo, pp. 116. Black cloth boards lettered

in gold on spine and front. Contents include all poems in No. 3, and twenty more. 2,000 copies printed.

8   THE EARTH COMPELS poems by Louis MacNeice. London: Faber & Faber (1938).
Poems. First edition, 8vo, pp. (4), 64. Brown cloth boards lettered in gold on spine. 3,640 copies printed.

9   I CROSSED THE MINCH by Louis MacNeice. Longmans, Green & Co., London, New York, Toronto (1938).
Prose, interspersed with a half-dozen poems. First edition, 8vo, pp. (4), 252. Eight drawings by Nancy Sharp. Black cloth boards lettered in gold on spine. 2,000 copies printed.

10   MODERN POETRY A Personal Essay by Louis MacNeice. Oxford University Press (1938).
Prose criticism. First edition, 4to, pp. (8), 208. Red cloth boards lettered in gold on spine. 2,000 copies printed.

10a ——— Second edition with an Introduction by Walter Allen. Oxford at the Clarendon Press, 1968.
Text as in No. 10, but 8vo, pp. (24), 208. Blue cloth boards lettered in gold on spine. 2,000 copies printed.

10b ——— American edition. New York: Haskell House, 1969.
Printed in U.S.A. Text and pagination as in No. 10 but gathered in 16's. Green cloth boards lettered in gold on spine.

11   ZOO. Louis MacNeice. London: Michael Joseph Ltd. (1938).
Prose. First edition, 8vo, pp. 256. Illustrations by Nancy Sharp. Green cloth boards lettered in silver on spine. 2,000 copies printed.

12   AUTUMN JOURNAL, a poem by Louis MacNeice. London: Faber & Faber (1939).
Poem. First edition, 8vo, pp. 96. Brown cloth boards lettered in gold on spine. 5,975 copies printed.

12a ——— American issue. New York: Random House, 1940.
Printed in Great Britain and identical with No. 12 except for title leaf and blue cloth boards lettered in gold on spine. 500 copies printed.

13   SELECTED POEMS by Lous MacNeice. London: Faber & Faber (1940).

Poems. First edition, 8vo, pp. 80. Blue paper-covered boards lettered in black on spine and front (in red on later impressions). 17,430 copies printed in several impressions.

14 THE LAST DITCH by Louis MacNeice. Dublin: The Cuala Press, 1940.
Poems. First edition, 4to, pp. (16), 40. Blue paper-covered boards with wide cloth spine, labelled on spine and lettered on front in black. 450 copies printed, (25 copies signed by author).

14a ———— Re-issue. Shannon: Irish University Press, 1971. pp. 33.

15 POEMS 1925 - 1940 by Louis MacNeice. New York: Random House (1941).
Poems. First edition, 8vo, pp. (16), 328. Blue cloth boards lettered in silver on spine. 2,005 copies printed.

16 THE POETRY OF W. B. YEATS. Louis MacNeice. Oxford University Press, London, New York, Toronto, 1941.
Prose criticism. First edition, 8vo, pp. (12), 244. Green cloth boards lettered in gold on spine. 3,500 copies printed.

16a ———— American edition. Oxford University Press, London, New York, Toronto (n.d.) [1941].
Printed in U.S.A. and identical with No. 16 except for pink cloth boards lettered in red on spine. 1,500 copies printed.

16b ———— Second edition with a foreward by Richard Ellmann. London: Faber & Faber (1967).
Faber paper covered edition, pp. 208. 7,000 copies printed.

16c ———— Second American edition. New York: Oxford University Press (1969).
O.U.P. Galaxy Book No. 269. Identical with No. 16b except for cover. 7,638 copies printed.

17 PLANT AND PHANTOM. Poems by Louis MacNeice. London: Faber & Faber (1941).
Poems. First edition, 8vo, pp. 88. Green cloth boards lettered in gold on spine. 4,088 copies printed.

18 MEET THE U.S. ARMY. London: His Majesty's Stationery Office (1943).
Prose. First edition, 12 sewn leaves, pp. 24. On p. 2 : 'written

for the Board of Education by Louis MacNeice.' Red paper cover decorated with white stars.

19 CHRISTOPHER COLUMBUS. A radio play. Louis Mac-Neice. London: Faber & Faber (1944).
Play. First edition, 8vo, pp. 29 Blue cloth boards lettered in gold on spine. 15,500 copies printed.

19a ———— Second edition. Faber School Editions (1963).
pp. 80. Olive cloth boards lettered in white on spine and front. 6,050 copies printed.

20 SPRINGBOARD. Poems 1941 - 1944. Louis MacNeice. London: Faber & Faber (1944).
Poems. First edition, 8vo, pp. 56. Orange cloth boards lettered in gold on spine. 7,000 copies printed.

20a ———— American edition. New York: Random House (1945). *Manufactured in U.S.A. pp. 64, gathered in 16's. Brown cloth boards lettered in gold on spine. 2,500 copies printed.*

21 THE DARK TOWER and other radio scripts by Louis Mac-Neice. London: Faber & Faber (1947).
Five plays for radio. First edition, 8vo, pp. 204. Grey cloth boards lettered in gold on spine. 4,000 copies printed.

21a ———— Re-issue. London: Faber paper-covered Edition (1964).
Reissue of pp. 9 to 66 of No. 21, i.e. of The Dark Tower *only. Pp. 62. 10,000 copies printed.*

22 HOLES IN THE SKY. Poems 1944 - 1947 by Louis MacNeice. London: Faber & Faber (1948).
Poems. First edition, 8vo, pp. 72. Blue cloth boards lettered in silver on spine. 2,650 copies printed.

22a ———— American edition. New York: Random House (1949).
Manufactured in U.S.A., 8vo, pp. 64. Brown cloth boards partly covered with cream paper bearing an olive leaf pattern, lettered in gold on spine. 2,000 copies printed.

23 COLLECTED POEMS 1925 - 1948 by Louis MacNeice. London: Faber & Faber (1949).
Poems. First edition, 8vo, pp. 312. Blue cloth boards lettered in gold on spine. 12,716 copies printed.

23a ———— American issue. New York: Oxford University Press (1963).
Printed in Great Britain and identical with No. 23 except on title page and spine. 869 copies printed.

24 GOETHE'S FAUST Parts I and II. An abridged version translated by Louis MacNeice. London: Faber & Faber (1951).
Verse play in translation. First edition, 8vo, pp. 308. Orange cloth boards lettered in gold on spine. 3,450 copies printed.

24a ———— American issue. New York: Oxford University Press, 1952.
Printed in Great Britain and identical with No. 24 except on title page and spine. 1,000 copies printed.

24b ———— American edition. New York: Oxford University Press, 1960.
O.U.P. Galaxy Book 45. pp. 312. Cream paper covers have a large dark brown illustration of Mephistopheles in full face, designed by Lorraine Blake. 105,102 copies printed in first fourteen impressions.

24c ———— Re-issue. London: Faber paper covered Edition (1965). *Identical with No. 24 except for title page including MacNeice's collaborator's name: E. L. Stahl, Taylor Professor of the German Language and Literature in the University of Oxford. 6,075 copies printed.*

25 TEN BURNT OFFERINGS by Louis MacNeice. London: Faber & Faber (1952).
Poems. First edition, 8vo, pp. 96. Pink cloth boards lettered in gold on spine. 3,000 copies printed.

25a ———— American issue. New York: Oxford University Press, 1953.
Printed in Great Britain and identical with No. 25 except on title page and spine.

26 THE PENNY THAT ROLLED AWAY. Louis MacNeice. New York: G. P. Putnam's Son, 1954.
Short story for children. First edition, 8vo, pp. 40. Illustrations by Marvin Bileck. Pink cardboard covers with pattern of one-cent coins lettered in black.

26a THE SIXPENCE THAT ROLLED AWAY by Louis Mac-
Neice. London: Faber & Faber (1956).
*British edition of No. 26, with title and names in the story
changed to British equivalents of American originals. 4to,
pp. 24. Illustrations by Edward Bawden. Blue paper-covered
boards, green cloth spine lettered in gold. 4,000 copies printed.*

27 THE OTHER WING by Louis MacNeice. London: Faber &
Faber (1954).
*Poem. First edition, pp. 4, sewn. An Ariel Poem, illustrated
by Michael Ayrton. Blue paper covers lettered in black. 5,130
copies printed.*

28 AUTUMN SEQUEL, A Rhetorical Poem in XXVI Cantos
by Louis MacNeice. London: Faber & Faber (1954).
*Poem. First edition, 8vo, pp. 164. Violet cloth boards lettered
in gold on spine. 4,000 copies printed.*

29 VISITATIONS by Louis MacNeice. London: Faber & Faber
(1957).
*Poems. First edition, 8vo, pp. 64. Blue cloth boards lettered in
gold on spine. 4,000 copies printed.*

29a ———— American issue. New York: Oxford University
Press, 1958.
*Printed in Great Britain and identical with No. 29 except on
title page and spine.*

30 EIGHTY-FIVE POEMS selected by the Author. Louis Mac-
Neice. London: Faber & Faber (1959).
*Poems. First edition, 8vo, pp. 128. Maroon cloth boards
lettered in white on spine. 3,000 copies printed.*

30a ———— American issue. New York: Oxford University Press
(1961).
*Printed in Great Britain and identical with No. 30 except on
title page and spine. 625 copies printed.*

31 SOLSTICES by Louis MacNeice. London: Faber & Faber
(1961).
*Poems. First edition, 8vo, pp. 80. Maroon cloth boards lettered
in gold. 3,200 copies printed.*

31a ———— American issue. New York: Oxford University Press,
1961.

Printed in Great Britain and identical with No. 31 except on title page and spine.

32   THE BURNING PERCH. Louis MacNeice. London: Faber & Faber (1963).
Poems. First edition, 8vo, pp. 60. Maroon cloth boards lettered in gold on spine. 7,060 copies printed.

32a ———— American issue. New York: Oxford University Press, 1963.
Printed in Great Britain and identical with No. 32 except on title page and spine. 780 copies printed.

33   THE MAD ISLANDS and THE ADMINISTRATOR. Two radio plays by Louis MacNeice. London: Faber & Faber (1964).
Two plays for radio. First edition, 8vo, pp. 112. Violet cloth boards lettered in gold on spine. 2,000 copies printed.

34   ASTROLOGY, Louis MacNeice. London: Aldus Books in association with W. H. Allen (1964).
Prose. First edition, 8vo, pp. 352. Black cloth boards lettered in gold on spine. Many photographs, drawings, and tables by various hands. 25,500 copies printed in several impressions. Also translated into French, German, Italian, and Spanish.

34a ———— American edition. New York: Doubleday & Company (1964).
Text and pagination identical with No. 34; slight differences in cover design. 76,000 copies printed in first seven impressions.

35   SELECTED POEMS OF LOUIS MacNEICE. Selected and introduced by W. H. Auden. London: Faber & Faber (1964).
Poems. First Faber paper covered edition, pp. 160. 22,000 copies printed.

36   THE STRINGS ARE FALSE. An Unfinished Autobiography by Louis MacNeice. London: Faber & Faber (1965).
Prose. First edition, 8vo, pp. 288. Edited by E. R. Dodds and with an appendix by John Hilton. Pink cloth boards lettered in gold on spine. 4,000 copies printed.

36a ———— American edition. New York: Oxford University Press, 1966.

Printed in U.S.A. Text and pagination identical with No. 36, but white cloth boards lettered in blue on spine. 3,075 copies printed.

37 VARIETIES OF PARABLE by Louis MacNeice. Cambridge at the University Press, 1965.
Prose criticism. First edition, 8vo, pp. (8), 160. Black cloth boards lettered in gold on spine. 5,000 copies printed.

38 THE COLLECTED POEMS OF LOUIS MacNEICE, edited by E. R. Dodds. London: Faber & Faber (1966).
Poems. First edition, 8vo, pp. (18), 578. Orange cloth boards lettered in gold on spine. 5,560 copies printed.

38a ———— American edition. New York: Oxford University Press, 1967.
Printed in U.S.A. Text as in No. 38, but two extra blank leaves, and all gathered in 16's. White cloth boards lettered in red and brown. 2,575 copies printed.

39 ONE FOR THE GRAVE. A modern morality play by Louis MacNeice. London: Faber & Faber (1968).
Play. First edition, 8vo, pp. 92. Blue cloth boards lettered in gold on spine, 4,050 copies printed.

39a ———— American issue. New York: Oxford University Press, 1968.
Printed in Great Britain and identical with No. 39 except on title page and spine. 1,796 copies printed.

40 PERSONS FROM PORLOCK and other plays for radio by Louis MacNeice with an Introduction by W. H. Auden. London: British Broadcasting Corporation (1969).
Four plays for radio. First edition, pp. 144, gathered in 16's. Green cloth boards lettered in gold on spine. 2,500 copies printed.

RADIO SCRIPTS 1941-1963

R. D. SMITH

This list is probably not quite inclusive or perfectly accurate since there are gaps and ambiguities in the cataloguing of the early years, and many scripts are, at the time of writing, unavailable for checking as they are being microfilmed.

My thanks to an old friend, Miss Kay Hutchings, Play Librarian, Drama (Radio), and a newer one, her assistant, the poet Nicholas Willey for their patient and gay assistance in compiling this list.

The dates are the dates of first transmission. Some scripts were broadcast both in the BBC Home and World (Overseas) Services: and also the programmes put out on short-wave were, of course, repeated several times to different Overseas areas, according to the time of the different services. Devil a bit of use there'd be sending to Australia, or America, or Asia, or Africa when the people there were asleep. 'The huntsmen are up in America, and they are already past their first sleep in Persia', so as this opening page of a working script shows, to get world coverage the BBC has to use several repeated transmissions. Repeat transmissions are not listed.

'THE STONES CRY OUT' — No. 26

To be recorded in Belfast: Sunday, 26th October 1700-1730.
Reproduction dates: 27th October 1515-1530 BST Eastern.
　　　　　　　　　　27/28th October 0315-0330 BST
　　　　　　　　　　　　　　N. American.
　　　　　　　　　　29th October 0945-1000 BST Pacific.
　　　　　　　　　　2nd November 2045-2100 BST African.

ANNOUNCER　This is London Calling.
　　　　　　We present now 'The Stones Cry Out' No. 26, the twenty-sixth of a weekly series of programmes constructed round buildings in London and other parts of Britain which have suffered damage or destruction from German bombs —

[141]

'THE STONES CRY OUT'

Fade up Liszt 'Les Preludes'
Hold. And to background for

SPEAKER 1   This is the first programme in this series dealing with Northern Ireland.

SPEAKER 2   In the spring of 1941 Northern Ireland suffered severe air raids.

SPEAKER 1   In the Northern Ireland capital, Belfast, there was heavy destruction of property.

Music out

SPEAKER 2   Belfast is a great industrial city —

SPEAKER 1   It leads the world in the manufacture of linen,

SPEAKER 2   It is famous for the building of ships,

SPEAKER 1   But of buildings destroyed in Belfast we have chosen a worker's home —

SPEAKER 2   One of many such houses — a humble house in a humble street.

SPEAKER 1   The stones cry out.

SPEAKER 2   But the people stand firm.

SPEAKER 1   We present A HOME IN BELFAST.

1941
Twenty scripts, mainly produced by colleagues Douglas Clevedon, Francis Dillon, E. A. Harding, Lawrence Gilliam and Stephen Potter.

15 February (General Overseas Service) WORD FROM AMERICA.
5 March (World) THE STONES CRY OUT:
    No. 1: DR. JOHNSON TAKES IT.
25 March (World) COOK'S TOUR OF THE LONDON SUBWAYS.
    (G.O.S.) NEWS FROM PLYMOUTH.
16 April (G.O.S.) THE MARCH OF THE 10,000.
26 May (World) THE STONES CRY OUT:
    No. 4: WESTMINSTER ABBEY.
2 June (World) THE STONES CRY OUT: No. 5:
    MADAME TUSSAUD'S.
13 June (Home) ARE THERE ANY RULES? (Discussion with L. A. G. Strong).
23 June (World) THE STONES CRY OUT: No. 8: ST. PAUL'S.

7 July (World) THE STONES CRY OUT:
   No. 10: THE HOUSE OF COMMONS.
16 July (Empire) FREEDOM FERRY:
   No. 10: LIFE ON AN EX-AMERICAN DESTROYER.
1 September (World) THE STONES CRY OUT:
   No. 18: THE TEMPLE.
6 September (Home) DR. CHEKOV.
29 September (World) THE STONES CRY OUT:
   No. 22: ROYAL COLLEGE OF SURGEONS.
27 October (World) THE STONES CRY OUT:
   No. 26: A HOME IN BELFAST.
28 October (Home) THE GLORY THAT IS GREECE.
24 November (World) THE STONES CRY OUT:
   No. 30: THE BARBICAN, PLYMOUTH.
9 December (Home) ALEXANDER NEVSKY.
30 December (Home) THE ROGUE'S GALLERY.
31 December (Home) SALUTE TO THE NEW YEAR.

1942
Seventeen scripts, about half of them produced by the author. Other producers were Malcolm Baker-Smith; D. G. Bridson; John Glyn-Jones; E. A. Harding; Royston Morley; Stephen Potter and Walter Rilla.

12 March (Home) VIENNA, THE TALE OF A CITY THAT NEVER DIES.
22 March (Home) SALUTATION TO GREECE.
1 April (World) CALLING ALL FOOLS.
12 April (Home) SALUTE TO THE U.S.S.R.
10 May (Home) THE DEBATE CONTINUES.
14 May (Home) BLACK GALLERY No. 1: DR. JOSEPH GOEBBELS.
14 June (G.O.S.) SALUTE TO THE UNITED NATIONS.
30 June (Home) THE UNDEFEATED.
16 July (Home) BLACK GALLERY No. 10: ADOLPH HITLER.
6 September (Home) THE UNITED NATIONS: A TRIBUTE.
25 September (Forces) HALFWAY HOUSE.
27 September (Home) HOMAGE TO STALINGRAD.
4 October (G.O.S.) SALUTE TO THE U.S. ARMY.
11 October (G.O.S.) BRITAIN TO AMERICA: THE COMMANDOS.
12 October (Home) CHRISTOPHER COLUMBUS.
22 October (Forces) THEY SHALL RISE AGAIN:
   No. 10: NANKING.
25 October (Home) SALUTE TO GREECE.

1943
Nineteen scripts, mainly produced by the author.

3 January (Home) SALUTE TO THE UNITED NATIONS.
29 January (G.O.S.) TWO MEN AND AMERICA.
21 February (Home) THE FOUR FREEDOMS: No. 1: PERICLES.
28 February (Home) THE FOUR FREEDOMS:
   No. 2: THE EARLY CHRISTIANS.
7 March (Home) THE FOUR FREEDOMS:
   No. 3: THE RENAISSANCE.
14 March (Home) THE FOUR FREEDOMS:
   No. 4: JOHN MILTON.
21 March (Home) THE FOUR FREEDOMS:
   No. 5: THE FRENCH REVOLUTION.
25 March (Home) LONG LIVE GREECE.
28 March (Home) THE FOUR FREEDOMS: No. 6: WHAT NOW?
19 April (G.O.S.) THE DEATH OF BYRON.
3 May (Home) ZERO HOUR.
18 June (Home) SICILY AND FREEDOM.
21 June (Home) THE DEATH OF MARLOWE.
4 July (Home) INDEPENDENCE DAY.
3 September (Home) FOUR YEARS AT WAR.
8 October (Home) THE STORY OF MY DEATH.
8 November (Home) THE SPIRIT OF RUSSIA:
   MUSIC, RIMSKY-KORSAKOV.
17 November (G.O.S.) THE FIFTH FREEDOM.
31 December (Home) RING IN THE NEW.

1944
Ten scripts, mainly produced by the author.

7 January (Home) THE SACRED BAND.
13 March (Home) THE NOSEBAG.
23 April (Home) THIS BREED OF MEN.
30 May (Home) D. DAY.
28 June (Home) HE HAD A DATE.
16 July (Home) SUNBEAMS IN HIS HAT.
13 August (Home) WHY BE A POET?
3 November (Home) THE GOLDEN ASS (ADAPTATION).
7 November (Home) CUPID AND PSYCHE.
31 December (Home) THE YEAR IN REVIEW.

1945
Five scripts, all produced by the author.

10 January (Home) A ROMAN HOLIDAY.
29 March (Home) THE MARCH HARE RESIGNS.
18 May (Home) LONDON VICTORIOUS.
22 May (Home) A VOICE FROM NORWAY.
31 December (Home) THRESHOLD OF THE NEW.

1946

Ten programmes scripted, seven produced by the author, and two by John Arlott.

21 January (Home) THE DARK TOWER.
1 April (Home) SALUTE TO ALL FOOLS.
14 June (Home) POETRY PROMENADE:
   No. 14: LOUIS MacNEICE (Selected by Phoebe Pool).
20 September (Third) ENTER CAESAR.
22 October (Third) THE CAREERIST.
29 October (Third) THE *AGAMEMNON* OF AESCHYLUS (translation).
2 November (Eastern) BOOK OF VERSE:
   No. 108: LOUIS MacNEICE (selection by Cecil Day Lewis).
16 November (Eastern) BOOK OF VERSE: No. 110: W. H. AUDEN (Selection by Louis MacNeice).
3 December (Third) ENEMY OF CANT.
13 December (Home) THE HEARTLESS GIANT.

1947

Five scripts, all produced by the author.

11 March (Third) THE DEATH OF GUNNAR.
12 March (Third) THE BURNING OF NJAL.
22 June (Home) PORTRAIT OF ROME.
27 July (Third) GRETTIR THE STRONG.
21 October (Third) AUTUMN JOURNAL (selections, and an extract from the Preface of the Poem).

1948

Six scripts, all produced by the author.

13 March (Third) INDIA AT FIRST SIGHT.
2 May (Home) INDIA AND PAKISTAN:
   No. 3: PORTRAIT OF DELHI.
23 May (Home) INDIA AND PAKISTAN:
   No. 6: THE ROAD TO INDEPENDENCE.
19 July (Third) THE TWO WICKED SISTERS.
19 September (Home) NO OTHER ROAD (United Nations).
22 December (Third) TRIMALCHIO'S FEAST (adaptation).

1949

Seven scripts, all but one produced by the author.

14 February (Third) HE HAD A DATE (revised text).
28 March (Third) THE QUEEN OF AIR AND DARKNESS.

26 August (Third) LOUIS MacNEICE READS HIS OWN POEMS (Produced, Frank Hauser).
30 October (Third) FAUST (translated, with E. L. Stahl) PART ONE.
31 October (Third) FAUST (translated, with E. L. Stahl) PART ONE CONCLUDED.
10 November (Third) FAUST (translated, with E. L. Stahl) PART TWO.
17 November (Third) FAUST (translated, with E. L. Stahl) PART TWO CONCLUDED.

1950
Absent in Greece.

1951
Absent in Greece till July: thereafter four scripts, all produced by the author.

15 September (Third) BURNT OFFERINGS (poems).
18 November (Home) PORTRAIT OF ATHENS.
11 December (Third) IN SEARCH OF ANOYIA.
18 December (Third) BURNT OFFERINGS (second series).

1952
Three scripts, all produced by the author.
28 January (Third) THE CENTRE OF THE WORLD: (DELPHI).
8 February (All services) MOURNING AND CONSOLATION (compilation).
9 November (Third) ONE EYE WILD.

1953
Three scripts, all produced by the author.

6 January (Home) TWELVE DAYS OF CHRISTMAS.
31 May (Home) TIME HAS BROUGHT ME HITHER.
5 July (Home) RETURN TO ATLANTIS.

1954
Nine scripts all produced by the author.

16 March (Home) WHERE NO WOUNDS WERE (adapted from the novel by Goronwy Rees).
27 April (Third) PRISONER'S PROGRESS.
28 June to 1 August (Third) AUTUMN SEQUEL (six parts).
15 October (Home) RETURN TO A SCHOOL (MARLBOROUGH).

1955
Four scripts, two produced by the author.

18 March (Third) THE WAVES (adaptation of the novel by Virginia Woolf).
19 March THE WAVES (contd.).
3 July (Home) THE FULLNESS OF THE NILE.
25 December (Home and Overseas) THE STAR WE FOLLOW (with Ritchie Calder): chief producer, Laurance Gilliam.

1956
Six scripts, all produced by the author.

5 February (Third) ALSO AMONG THE PROPHETS (SAUL).
2 May ON THE RIGHTS OF MAN.
17 June (Home) BOW BELLS.
29 July (Home) SPIRES AND GANTRIES: (ROUEN).
8 October (Third) CARPE DIEM.
30 December (Home) FROM BARD TO BUSKER.

1957
Four scripts, all produced by the author.

27 May (Home) NUTS IN MAY.
        (Home) THE BIRTH OF GHANA.
22 September (Home) AN OXFORD ANTHOLOGY.
24 September (Home) THE STONES OF OXFORD.

1958
Three scripts, all produced by the author.

9 January (Third) BORDER BALLADS (compilation).
1 April (Home) ALL FOOLS AT HOME.
7 April (Home) HEALTH IN THEIR HANDS (U.N.O. on World Health).

1959
Six scripts, all produced by the author.

11 January (Third) NEW POETRY.
3 April (Home) SCRUMS AND DREAMS (Cardiff Arms Park).
25 July (Third) EAST OF THE SUN AND WEST OF THE MOON.
8 November (Third) POEMS BY TENNYSON (compiled with comments).
8 December (Third) THEY MET ON GOOD FRIDAY.
30 December (Home) MOSAIC OF YOUTH (compilation).

1960

Thirteen scripts, all produced by the author.

> 6 October to 22 December (Third) THE ODYSSEY (adapted in 12 parts) PART 3 HADES he also translated.
> (Third) MEDIEVAL LATIN POETS (compiled with comments).

1961

MacNeice went on a half-time contract. Four scripts, all produced by the author.

> 10 March (Third) THE ADMINISTRATOR.
> 6 November (Third) POEMS BY QUASIMODO (introduced).
> 14 November (Third) ONE EYE WILD (revised).
> 19 December (Third) LET'S GO YELLOW.

1962

One script, produced by the author.

> 4 April (Third) THE MAD ISLANDS.

1963

Four scripts, all produced by the author.

> 24 March (Third) LATIN POETRY.
> 9 June (Third) NEW POETRY (introduced).
> 11 August (Third) MEDIEVAL LATIN POETRY.
> 30 August (Third) PERSONS FROM PORLOCK.

CONTRIBUTORS

WALTER ALLEN. Born in Birmingham 1911. Educated Birmingham University. Among many publications are his novel *All in a Lifetime*, a critical study *Tradition and Dream*, and *Transatlantic Crossing : American visitors to Britain and British visitors to Amerca in the Nineteenth Century*. Professor Allen has taught in universities in Britain, Ireland and the United States. He is currently Professor of English Literature, Dalhousie University, Nova Scotia.

KEVIN ANDREWS. Born in Peking 1924. Educated Harvard University. Has published *Castles of the Morea, The Flight of Ikaros, Athens* (Cities of the World No. 7) and, in 1974, a long poem, *First Will and Testament*. Mr. Andrews lives in Athens.

CHRISTOPHER M. ARMITAGE. Educated at the Universities of Oxford, Western Ontario and Duke University, North Carolina. Has published (with Neil Clark) *A Bibliography of the Works of Louis MacNeice* and is writing the monograph *Louis MacNeice* for the Bucknell University Press series on Irish Writers.

W. H. AUDEN. Born in England in 1907. Among many publications were *Letters from Iceland* (with Louis MacNeice). Sometime Professor of Poetry in the University of Oxford. In his lifetime the late W. H. Auden won many honours for his poetry, among them King George's Gold Medal for Poetry and the Pulitzer Prize. He was a member of the American Academy of Arts and Letters.

DALLAS GORDON BOWER. Born London 1907. Trained with Marconi Scientific Instrument Co. Ltd. and British Thomson Houston. Was Assistant Editor, and for a short period Editor, *The Wireless Engineer*. Entered British film production 1928 and the BBC television service 1936. Has produced and directed many BBC television productions, including *Tristan and Isolde, Julius Caesar, The Tempest, The Taming of the Shrew*, etc. BBC sound radio wartime productions include *Alexander Nevsky* and *Christopher Columbus*.

E. R. DODDS. Born in Ireland in 1893. Sometime Regius Professor of Greek in the University of Oxford. Among his many publications are *Journal and Letters of Stephen MacKenna, The Greeks and the Irrational, Pagan and Christian in an Age of Anxiety*, and *Thirty-Two Poems*. Professor Dodds is editor of *The Collected Poems of Louis MacNeice*, and of MacNeice's unfinished autobiography, *The Strings are False*.

CORINNA MacNEICE. Born in London 1943. Educated in Athens, Switzerland, London and at the Slade School of Fine Art. Since then has painted, taught and lived in London and held exhibitions of painting and drawing in Oxford, Belfast, Dublin and London.

[149]

DEREK MAHON. Born in Ireland in 1941. Educated at Trinity College, Dublin. Has published two books of poems, *Night Crossing* and *Lives*. Is editor of *The Sphere Book of Modern Irish Poetry*, was a founding editor of *Atlantis*, and has won the Gregory Award for his poetry.

LIAM MILLER. Born in Ireland in 1924. Educated at University College, Dublin. Founded the Dolmen Press in 1951, and is a Director of the Cuala Press. Has edited *Retrospect*. Mr. Miller is lecturer on book production in the Library School, University College, Dublin, and has served as Chairman of Irish PEN and as President of the Yeats Association. He is President of the Irish Book Publishers' Association.

JOHN MONTAGUE. Born in New York in 1929. Educated at University College, Dublin, and Yale University. Lecturer in English Literature at University College, Cork. Among his publications are *Poisoned Lands, A Chosen Light, Tides, The Rough Field*, and *Death of a Chieftain and Other Stories*. Has written many literary essays and was editor of *The Faber Book of Irish Verse*.

CAROLINE ELIZABETH NICHOLSON. Eldest child of the late Right Revd. John Frederick MacNeice. Born in East Belfast in 1903. Educated at Sherborne School for Girls, St. Hugh's College, Oxford, and Charing Cross Hospital Medical School. Married to Sir John Nicholson, F.R.C.S., who is a consulting surgeon.

BERNARD SHARE. Born in 1930. Educated at Trinity College, Dublin. Sometime lecturer in English Literature, Newcastle University College, New South Wales. Publications include *The Moon is Upside Down, Inish, Merciful Hours, Irish Lives*, and books for children. Mr. Share is Secretary of the Irish Book Publishers' Association.

ROBIN SKELTON. Born in England in 1925. Educated at the Universities of Cambridge and Leeds. Professor of English Literature in the University of Victoria, British Columbia. Among many publications are *Patmos and Other Poems, The Dark Window, Selected Poems, An Irish Album*, and *The Poetic Pattern*. Mr. Skelton is a Fellow of the Royal Society of Literature.

R. D. SMITH. BBC writer/producer for many years; also theatre producer. Formerly Acting Deputy Postmaster-General, Government of Palestine, latterly winner of Italia Prize for Radio. Now Professor in the New University of Ulster, at the Post-graduate Institute of Continuing Education in Derry. Married for 35 years to Irish novelist Olivia Manning.

E. L. STAHL. Born in South Africa in 1902. Sometime Taylor Professor of the German Language and Literature in the University of Oxford. Among his many publications are editions of Goethe's *Werther* and Rilke's *Duino Elegies, The Dramas of Heinrich von Kleist*, and the revised *Oxford Book of German Verse*. Professor Stahl collaborated with Louis MacNeice in the translation of Goethe's *Faust*.

W. B. STANFORD. Born in Ireland in 1910. Regius Professor of Greek, Trinity College, Dublin. Publications include *Greek Metaphor, Aeschylus in his Style, The Ulysses Theme,* and *The Sound of Greek.* He has also published articles on classical, political and ecclesiastical topics and some poems.

ANTHONY THWAITE. Born in England in 1930. Educated Christ Church, Oxford. His publications include *The Owl in the Tree, The Stones of Emptiness, Inscriptions, New Confessions, Contemporary English Poetry* and *Poetry Today.* Mr. Thwaite has lectured in universities in Japan, Libya and Kuwait, has been a radio producer in the Features Department of the BBC, has been literary editor of *The Listener* and of the *New Statesman.* Currently is co-editor of *Encounter.* Mr. Thwaite won the Richard Hillary Prize in 1968.